TREES
AND SHRUBS

LINDA GAMLIN

HAMLYN

HOW TO USE THIS BOOK

**MIDLAND
HAWTHRON**
*Crataegus
oxyacanthoides*
Ll2–6cm. Rarer than
common hawthorn.
Look at the leaf shape, and
underneath the leaf – there
are no tufts of hair where
the veins branch from the
central vein.

This guide covers over 200 species of tree
and shrub, many of which can be observed
in the UK. The identification pages
(44–125) give the common English name,
followed by the scientific name in italics.
To help in recognizing the trees, the leaf
length (Ll) is given in centimetres and
millimetres for each individual entry.
However, leaves can often be variable in
length, e.g. young trees or shoots may
have much longer leaves than the adult.
Some trees may also have more than one
sort of leaf (e.g. cypress and eucalyptus).
The leaf measurement is for the adult leaf
unless otherwise stated, and should be
used for a guide only.

The author and editor would like to thank the
following individuals for their assistance in the
preparation of this book: Andrew Branson of
British Wildlife Publishing, Principal Consultant
and Sarah Castell and Mei Lim, Designers.

Published in 1993 by
Hamlyn Children's Books,
part of Reed Children's Books Ltd.,
Michelin House, 81 Fulham Road,
London SW3 6RB

ISBN 0 600 57380 X

Printed in Hong Kong

Series designer: Nick Leggett

SAFETY CODE

- **DO NOT GO TO FORESTS AND WOODS ALONE.**

- **ALWAYS TELL AN ADULT WHERE YOU ARE GOING, AND WHEN YOU WILL BE BACK.**

- **NEVER EAT THE BERRIES, FRUITS, NUTS, LEAVES OR ROOTS OF ANY TREE OR SHRUB UNLESS YOU ARE SURE IT IS SAFE TO DO SO.**

- **TREAT ALL WILDLIFE WITH RESPECT.**

- **DO NOT DRINK WATER FROM A RIVER OR POND.**

CONTENTS

ABOUT TREES

A forest in Sweden with a mixture of conifers, such as pines, and broadleaved trees such as birches, aspens and rowans. Forests like this are called 'mixed forests'.

TREE DIFFERENCES

Birds, bats, roses, grasses and trees – which is the odd one out? The answer is 'trees' because they are not a single group of related living things, as each of the other groups is. A tree is just a very tall plant, and one tree may be no more like another tree than a giraffe is like a frog. So why do trees all look so similar? In fact, when you look closely, there are plenty of differences – a palm tree, an oak and a fir tree have little in common, apart from a long trunk. Trees evolved many times over millions of years, to beat other plants in the competition for sunlight, the source of all their food. For a plant to get its leaves high up above the ground there is really only one shape for it – tall, with a long stalk (trunk) to keep the leaves aloft. This is what we mean by a 'tree'.

A shrub or a tree? The difference is that trees have a single thick woody stem, called the trunk, whereas shrubs, such as this guelder rose have several woody stems. A tree also has to reach a certain height to qualify – usually about 6 metres (20 feet).

1. You can collect tree seeds and grow them in pots. Choose any tree that produces plenty of seeds – acorns, beechnuts, sycamore seeds or conkers are all good. Mix the seeds with damp sand and leave outdoors in a pot for the winter.

2. The seeds need a period of cold before they can germinate. (Some, such as ash, need 18 months of cold.) In the spring, plant them in potting compost or light soil. Plant three to each pot, and take out the weakest seedlings later.

3. If you have several seedlings, you can afford to dig some up at various stages to see how they grow. Make drawings or photographs of each stage so that you have a series of pictures of how a young tree develops from its seed.

The fir tree is a typical conifer, with its 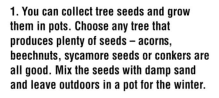 triangular outline and needle-like leaves. The seeds are produced inside woody cones.

The oak is a broadleaved tree. Unlike a conifer, the topmost bud of the tree does not suppress the growth of side-buds, so large side-branches can develop, giving the tree a more rounded shape.

HOW THEY GROW

Leaves have holes on the underside to take in carbon dioxide and oxygen.

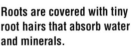

Branches fall off, leaving eye-like marks on trunks, and knots in the wood.

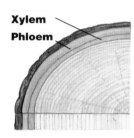

Xylem

Phloem

Xylem vessels conduct water up the stem, phloem vessels take sugary sap downwards.

Roots are covered with tiny root hairs that absorb water and minerals.

GROWTH PATTERNS

The roots of a tree absorb water and minerals (such as nitrogen and iron) from the soil. These flow up the trunk to the branches and leaves. The leaves absorb sunlight and carbon dioxide and turn them into food, in the form of sugar. The sugar flows back down the trunk to feed the roots, in a syrupy liquid called sap. The growing points of the tree are at the tips of the branches, and in a layer all around the trunk just below the bark. So the trunk gradually gets fatter as this layer grows, while the tree gets taller because the branches grow. If you tie a swing to the lower branches of a tree it does not get higher every year, because the trunk is not getting any taller (except at the very tip which is still growing in some trees, notably conifers).

Bark is a thick corky layer that protects the tree trunk. As the trunk gets fatter, it outgrows the bark, and the outer layer of bark cracks.

All the important parts of ▼ the trunk are just below the bark. The centre of a tree trunk is dead wood, and serves little purpose apart from support, which is why hollow trees survive.

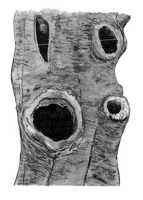

Tree trunks grow fast in ▲ spring, slower in summer and not at all in winter. Each 'tree ring' is a layer of soft spring wood with a layer of hard summer wood outside it.

Thin young branches are ▲ pulled down by their own weight as they grow. To compensate, they curve upwards again, by growing more on the underside than on the top.

TREE-SPOTTING

Look out for trees that have been ▼ shaped by their environment. The top of this hawthorn has been regularly nibbled by cows, and it has grown very low and wide as a result.

This seaside hawthorn has not ▲ been bent by the wind as you might think. Buds on one side are killed by the salty wind, while buds on the sheltered side survive, producing growth on that side only.

LOOKING AT LEAVES

All leaves have an important job to do. They make the tree's food by a process called photosynthesis. This uses the energy in sunlight to turn carbon dioxide gas (which the leaves get from the air around them) into sugar. Leaves are green because the chemical that makes photosynthesis possible, called chlorophyll, is always green. Some leaves are tough and leathery to keep leaf-eating insects at bay. Many contain resins and other unpleasant chemicals for the same reason, particularly conifers. The trees that lose their leaves every winter – called deciduous trees – can afford to have more delicate leaves, because if they are damaged it does not matter so much. Conifers have slender needle-like or strap-like leaves to allow the snow to fall off them easily, because they stay on the tree all winter.

Look up through a tree, and you will see very little sky – the leaves are arranged to catch all the light, but not to overlap each other much.

Ash
Leaves that are divided in this way are called 'pinnate'.

Holly
Holly leaves are prickly, leathery and waxy.

Larch
Larches have thin, needle-like leaves, in whorls.

Cypress
Cypress leaves are tiny scales pressed tight against the stem.

Pine
Pine needles are long and usually very hard.

Hazel
Some trees, such as hazel, have very variable leaves.

You may find leaf skeletons in the leaf litter of woods. They are formed when most of the leaf rots away, but the veins, which are slightly tougher, do not. You can make leaf skeletons and so compare the vein structure of different tree types. Ask an adult to help you as the caustic soda you will use can damage your skin. Dissolve a teaspoon of caustic soda in a pint of water, and let the leaves soak in it overnight. If nothing has happened after two days, make up a stronger solution of caustic soda and try again. Remove and rinse the skeletons when they have formed, and lay them out to dry.

Dead leaves soon curl up and become unrecognizable. Pressing avoids this by making them dry flat. Lay the leaves out singly on a sheet of blotting paper or kitchen roll. Place another sheet on top, then pile up several books so that they press down hard on the leaves. The leaves will be dry within two weeks. You can then stick them in your record book, with a leaf skeleton from the same tree alongside each one, so that you can compare the vein pattern with the overall shape of the leaf.

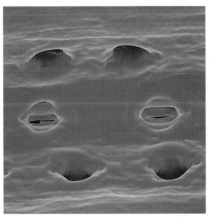

Identifying trees is not always easy, and learning to inspect leaves carefully can help. Always crush a leaf between your fingers and sniff — not all have a smell, but many do, and this can be useful if you get to know them. Feel the leaf carefully, as the texture is important, and look for tiny hairs, especially underneath the leaf. A hand-lens is useful for this. This is a Norway spruce needle, magnified 175 times.

FLOWER WATCHING

Like all plants, trees need to set seed. The seeds are carried away from the tree and grow into new young trees. In this way, when the parent tree dies it has left some offspring behind, carrying its genes. Seeds are the offspring of two different parent trees. One provides the male cells (in the form of pollen) and the other the female cells. For this to happen, pollen has to travel from one tree to another. In some species it is blown by the wind, in others it is carried by insects. The trees that use insects have colourful flowers, often quite large, to attract the insects' attention. They may also be scented for the same reason. Wind-pollinated trees often produce their flowers in catkins which contain hundreds of tiny flowers packed closely together.

In general, green flowers are wind-pollinated, but this is not always true. Maple flowers such as these from Père David's maple, are usually pollinated by insects which they attract by scent.

The earliest flowering plants were insect-pollinated and looked rather like magnolias. In time, some developed into wind-pollinated plants, probably so that they could flower at a time when few insects were about. Willows are interesting because they were previously wind-pollinated, and still have the catkins to prove it, but they are largely pollinated by insects. These flowers are making the return trip, evolving from wind pollination to insect pollination.

Horse chestnut flowers

Birch catkins

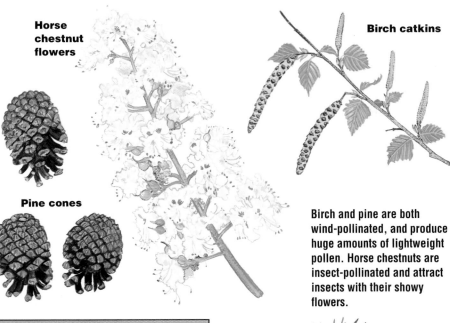

Pine cones

Birch and pine are both wind-pollinated, and produce huge amounts of lightweight pollen. Horse chestnuts are insect-pollinated and attract insects with their showy flowers.

PROJECT

Willows are often pollinated by moths. If you have a willow tree near your home, or in your garden, spread a sheet under it at night, when it is in flower, and shake the tree. The moths will fall from the tree onto the sheet below. Using a torch, you will be able to see all the moths that have been attracted to the flowers.

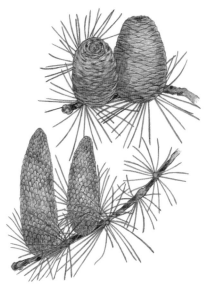

Unlike flowering plants, conifers and their ancestors have always been wind-pollinated. The abundant pollen is produced by male cones, which are smaller than the female cones. They shrivel and drop off after the pollen has dispersed.

SPOTTING SEEDS AND NUTS

Autumn is the easiest time of year for learning to recognize trees. You could begin by making a collection of seeds, fruits or nuts.

DISTRIBUTION

Trees need to get their seeds as far away from them as possible, so that their offspring do not start growing beneath their canopy. Many seeds do sprout up there, but soon die off. The lucky seeds are the ones which get away. Some are blown away by the wind, from trees such as maples and ashes. Other species rely on animals to transport their seeds. Many of these have tasty fruits which are eaten by birds. The hard seeds are inside the fruits and the birds deposit them unharmed in their droppings. Nuts are unusual seeds because the tree actually benefits by an animal eating them. They are large, nutritious and long-lasting, which appeals to animals such as squirrels who store them for the winter. Many nuts are buried and some are forgotten. These can grow and thrive.

Squirrels eat many nuts, but they rarely remember all the places where they have buried them. So nut-bearing trees get a skilled planting service, not just dispersal, from their animal helpers.

Tree fruits and nuts are an ▷
important part of our diet as
well. Most of those we eat
today have been altered by
plant breeders so that the
fruits are sweeter and juicier,
the nuts less bitter.

Date

Pear

Apple

Peach

Pomegranate

◁ Tree seeds are often very
nutritious, because a young
tree needs a good supply of
food to get started. Mice,
voles, jays, nuthatches and
other animals all feast on
seeds in the autumn, so look
for their feeding signs.

PROJECT

How far can the wind scatter a tree's
seeds? You can find out for yourself by
choosing a tree such as an ash, sycamore,
silver birch, white willow or hornbeam.
Find one that is growing alone, far from
others of its kind. First learn to identify its
seedlings, by growing the seeds yourself
or by looking carefully under the tree.
Some examples are shown here to help
you. Now work out from the tree, looking
for seedlings. Repeat on all sides of the
tree. If there is a strong prevailing wind the
seeds may go further in that direction.

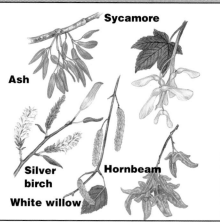

Sycamore

Ash

**Silver
birch**

Hornbeam

White willow

THE LIFE OF A TREE

Trees do not always grow at the same rate. Some, such as the holm oak shown here, grow very slowly in their first decade, then speed up later.

AN OAK'S LONG LIFE

Is there an old oak tree near where you live? Oak trees can live for up to 800 years. If it had eyes and ears, imagine all the changes such a tree would have seen during its long life. The invention of the motor car and the aeroplane would seem like very recent events – for most of its life it would only have seen people on foot, on horseback or in horse-drawn carts. Many of the large trees you see in parks or on housing estates were there hundreds of years ago, in completely different circumstances, and new buildings, roads or parkland have been created around them. Try to find old pictures of your neighbourhood – libraries, secondhand bookshops or local history societies are good places to start – and look closely for the trees. Can you recognize any still standing today?

The oldest trees in the world are the bristlecone pines, found high up in the Rocky Mountains of America. Scientists can now look at their growth rings without chopping them down, and they estimate that some are 6,000 years old.

Adopt a tree, choosing one near you that you like, and keep a record of its life for a few years.

Estimate the height of the tree using a ruler, with a friend standing beside the tree. Measure the height of the tree and of your friend on the ruler.

Now measure your friend against a doorpost. The height of the tree can be worked out: if the tree was five times as tall as your friend when measured with the ruler, and your friend is one metre tall, then the tree is 5 metres tall.

Use a piece of string to measure around the trunk of the tree. Write down all these measurements and repeat them every year to see how fast the tree grows.

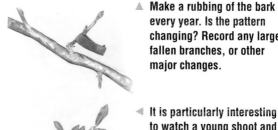

Make a rubbing of the bark every year. Is the pattern changing? Record any large fallen branches, or other major changes.

Estimate how many flowers and seeds are produced each year. Do the numbers vary much? You could take photographs of some typical branches to show how many flowers or seeds they carry.

It is particularly interesting to watch a young shoot and see how it slowly develops into an old twig or branch. Mark your chosen shoot with insulating tape so you can recognize it, and draw it twice a year.

TREE-SPOTTING IN WINTER

If you can identify deciduous trees in winter, when they have no leaves, you are a really expert tree-spotter. You need to look for the shape and colour of the twigs, the shape, size and colour of the buds, the arrangement of the buds on the twig, and the bark pattern (although this is very variable for some trees). Sometimes the tree shape is also helpful. But don't expect to be able to do this straight away. When you begin tree-spotting, even trees in leaf can be difficult. At first, only try to identify trees that have flowers, seeds, fruits or nuts on them. Once you've identified your tree, look carefully at the leaves, buds, twigs and bark. Try to remember the texture and smell (if any) of the leaves. Soon you will be able to identify trees with only leaves on, *and* trees without leaves.

A few trees can be identified from their trunk alone, such as the snake bark maples with their distinctive green-and-white striped bark.

As well as the bark, twigs and buds, look out for the remains of seeds and nuts still hanging on the tree, or just the seed stalks. Remember to look on the ground too.

Horse chestnut twigs have large crescent-shaped leaf-scars and sticky buds.

Tree of heaven twigs also have large leaf-scars, and many small pores.

Walnut has two types of bud: one produces leaves, the other produces flowers.

Ash buds are unmistakable: black and beautifully formed, on smooth grey twigs.

Manna ash has greyish buds shaped either like fat onions or bishop's mitres.

Cherry trees (and oaks) have their buds all clustered at the ends of the twigs.

PROJECT

Beech buds are shiny brown, smooth, long and slender, like bayonets or daggers.

It is easy to get lost in a wood, but if you know how to read the trees you may be able to find your way home. If you are in a place where the wind usually blows from the same direction, then one side of each tree trunk will be rained on more than the other, on average. This will encourage micro-scopic algae to grow on that side, giving it a greener colour.

Maples have their buds arranged opposite each other, in pairs along the twig.

Limes have their neat little buds placed alternately along smooth slender twigs.

RECORDING TREES

DRAWING AND PHOTOGRAPHING

Keeping a record of the species you see is a good way to build up your tree knowledge quickly. Try making drawings of the leaves, bark and twigs, because nothing makes you look so carefully as having to draw a picture. You will always be able to identify a tree in future if you have drawn it once. To photograph trees, you need to choose them carefully, especially if you want to take the whole tree. Look for a good vantage point where you can get it all into the picture – this is usually the most difficult part. Be prepared to wait until the sun comes round to just the right angle. Taking photographs in woods is more difficult, and you may need to buy special film (ASA 400) that is more sensitive to light, for use in dark conditions.

To take a picture like this, point the camera downwards, towards the sunlit leaves, to get the right setting. Switch the camera to manual, and set it according to the reading from the leaves.

Photographing leaves is ▷ tricky as they move about even when there is very little breeze. Get a friend to hold them steady, or go supplied with two or three clothes pegs. By pegging two or more twigs together you can still the movement, but be sure to keep the pegs out of the picture!

PROJECT

Choose a striking tree and photograph it at different seasons of the year. Take the spring photo when it is in flower.

Mark the spot where you take the photos with a large stone and take the next season, summer.

Choose a day with bright sun, or golden sunlit mist, to pick out the autumn colours of the leaves.

Snowy landscapes make a wonderful background for the stark winter silhouettes of trees.

FINDING UNUSUAL TREES

Botanic gardens and large parks, where the trees are labelled to show the species, can be interesting places to go tree-spotting. Try to identify the trees before you read the label – you may not be able to do so exactly, but you should be able to say, for example, if it is an oak, a rowan or a maple. Some of the trees you find there will be very unusual, and confusingly different from the trees you are used to. You may see varieties of beech and silver birch with ferny, divided leaves, for example, a variety of ash with large undivided leaves, or oaks with totally un-oak-like leaves. For this reason, parks with no labels are a bad place to start tree-spotting – wait until you have some expertise.

The Judas tree often produces flowers directly from the trunk and branches. Notice the shape of the flowers, which tell you that it belongs to the pea family.

Botanic gardens contain many different kinds of trees, often including unusual ones from distant parts of the world.

Even if you only have a small space available, you can still grow beautiful trees by learning the 'bonsai' method, invented in Japan, which produces miniature trees.

1. Start with a seedling tree and grow it in a shallow bowl with drainage material in the base.

2. In winter, allow the soil to dry out, dig up the tree and prune back the roots. Cut back the branches. This stunts the tree's growth and produces a tiny gnarled tree.

3. The Japanese like bonsais to have interesting twisty shapes, and to lean sideways. Use thick metal wire to train the branches and trunk in these shapes.

4. Keep your bonsai out of doors most of the time, as they dislike central heating. Water regularly in summer.

5. Set rocks around the trees to give a more picturesque effect. You can even train some of the roots over the rock.

SEEING TREES AROUND US

A hundred years ago, synthetic materials did not exist, and everything was made of natural products. Timber was enormously important then, and it is still widely used today. Some woods are very hard, others soft and easily worked. Most float on water, so they make good boats, but a few of the heavy, oily woods sink. Some of these are so durable they are used for breakwaters. Sometimes the names of woods tell you how they were used. The Romans valued the wood of box for making small oblong containers for precious items. They called these 'containers made of box' which gives us the word 'box' for a container.

Woods from conifers are called softwoods, while those from broadleaves are called hardwoods. Some softwoods are hard, however, and some hardwoods are very soft.

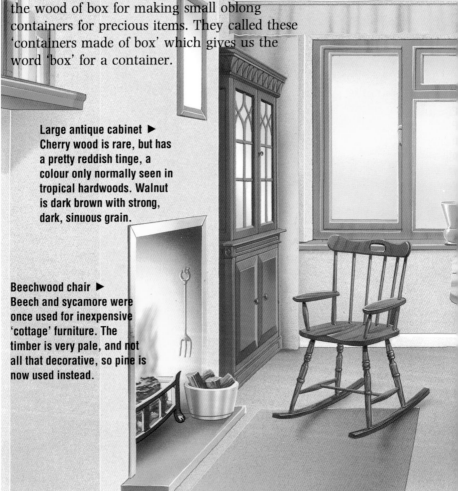

Large antique cabinet ▶
Cherry wood is rare, but has a pretty reddish tinge, a colour only normally seen in tropical hardwoods. Walnut is dark brown with strong, dark, sinuous grain.

Beechwood chair ▶
Beech and sycamore were once used for inexpensive 'cottage' furniture. The timber is very pale, and not all that decorative, so pine is now used instead.

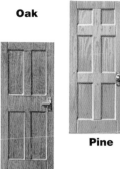

Oak

Cherry

Pine

Most hardwoods now come from tropical rainforests, which are largely destroyed to produce them. But they are not needed because today's softwoods are grown to very high standards, and soaked in fungicide if used for doors or windows. Learn to recognize tropical hardwoods: most have no growth rings, or only faint rings. They are often reddish, and have a fine close grain giving them a satiny look.

Pine dining table
Pine is a conifer so the wood it produces is a softwood, often called deal. Notice its yellowish colour, heavy growth-rings, and large knots.

Door-frame ▲
Doors and windows are often made of hardwoods from the disappearing tropical rainforests. Softwood doors and windows last just as long if painted carefully.

◄ **Modern pine dresser**
Knots appear where side-branches grew out from the trunk. If you look at conifers growing you will see many spindly side branches, which is why the wood is so knotty.

▲ **Oak chairs**
Oak is easily recognized by its short glossy streaks, paler than the rest, at right angles to the main grain. Old furniture is often made of oak.

PARKS AND GARDENS

Have you ever been to a tree zoo? You may think that you've never heard of such a thing, but you have. They are called parks. The largest ones contain hundreds of different trees from far distant lands. In general, identification is much more difficult here, unless the trees are labelled. Bear in mind that the tips given in this book for distinguishing tree species may not work if you find a really unusual tree. Like all identification rules, they work for a local area, not worldwide.

Willow-leaved pear ▼
A tree from southeast Europe and Central Asia that is guaranteed to confuse anyone but a tree expert.

◄ **Weeping ash**
An artificial variety of the ordinary hedgerow ash. The most dramatic of the weeping trees, throwing its branches into strange contorted poses.

◄ **Ornamental cherry**
An enormous number of different ornamental cherries have been bred, mostly in Japan. In spring, they are loaded down with blossom.

▲ **Red-flowered horse chestnut**
An artificial hybrid, but not very vigorous. Grown for the flowers, among the most beautiful of any tree.

▼ Ginkgo
From China, one of the strangest trees in the world. In a good year, older trees may produce flowers and fruit, but this is a rare event.

Copper beech ▼
A variety of the ordinary beech. It is often seen in the countryside too, where parkland has been 'landscaped'.

Box elder ▼
Box elder is neither a box nor an elder. It is a type of maple, but one with very unusual leaves.

◄ Ornamental crab-apple
These are artificial varieties, like the ornamental cherries, but grown as much for their pretty fruits as for blossom.

▲ Japanese maple
A wide range of leaf shapes and colours have been produced in the different varieties. See how many you can find.

Catalpa ▲
From North America. An odd tree, often having long snaky branches but very sparse leaves. Some of these leaves are huge.

STREETS AND ROADSIDES

Only certain species make good street trees. They need to be able to withstand both pollution and a heavy layer of tarmac or paving stones over their roots. Some trees, such as sycamores, are badly affected by this cramping of their roots. It weakens them so much that they become infested with scale insects (you can see these as white dots on the branches). Trees whose roots are strong enough to fight up through the pavement are not desirable either. Today's town planners usually like small, neat, well-behaved trees that develop the same predictable shape. Fastigiate trees, whose branches sweep upwards, are sometimes chosen.

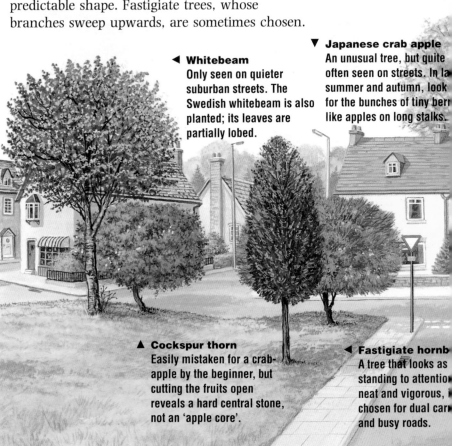

▼ Japanese crab apple
An unusual tree, but quite often seen on streets. In la summer and autumn, look for the bunches of tiny berr like apples on long stalks.

◄ Whitebeam
Only seen on quieter suburban streets. The Swedish whitebeam is also planted; its leaves are partially lobed.

▲ Cockspur thorn
Easily mistaken for a crab-apple by the beginner, but cutting the fruits open reveals a hard central stone, not an 'apple core'.

◄ Fastigiate hornb
A tree that looks as standing to attentio neat and vigorous, chosen for dual car and busy roads.

London plane ▼
An excellent street tree,
apart from the little golden
hairs that are shed along
with the seeds and irritate
the nose and throat.

▲ Italian alder
The leaves are dark and very
glossy. Look for next year's
catkins from late summer
onwards – they point
upwards like green candles.

▲ Purple-leaved plum
One of the earliest trees to
flower, with its leaves a pale
coppery green. In winter, it is
a mass of slender, black,
windswept twigs.

ANCIENT WOODLAND

Before human beings arrived, most of Europe was covered by forest. The earliest farmers began cutting it down with stone axes, and later generations made greater inroads with iron axes. There are only a few tiny fragments of the original forest, or 'wildwood', left. Those that remain have mostly been managed for centuries to provide useful timber, so they are not quite like the original forest. Even so, they are rich in different species of plants, butterflies and birds. The trees include oaks, ashes and hazels, sometimes mixed with more unusual species such as wild service tree and crab apple. The exact mix of trees depends on climate, soil, and how the wood has been managed in the past.

Hornbeam ▶
Usually a small tree, growing below the upper canopy of oak and ash. Such trees are known as the 'understorey'.

Hawthorn ▼
Rarely becoming a tree in woods, the hawthorn forms part of the shrub layer along with holly, blackthorn, hazel and guelder rose.

◀ Field maple
A pretty tree seen mostly in hedges but sometimes in ancient woods. This could be coppiced like hazel.

◄ Oak
Oak trees, particularly the Common oak, are very rich in insects – hundreds of species feed on them, which attracts insect-eating birds.

Jays like acorns and favour ancient forests. Look for the white rump and the blue flash of their wings as they fly off.

Small-leaved lime ▼
An unusual woodland tree. Very similar to the limes seen in gardens and roadsides, but with slightly smaller leaves.

◄ Ash
Lke oak and hornbeam, ash is common now because its wood was highly valued in the past. It was used for the handles of rakes, pitchforks and spades.

Coppiced hazel ▶
This was cut back to a stump every 2–3 years. The stump then produced long straight stems, used for fuel and fencing. Abandoned coppice like this is a common sight.

YOUNG WOODLAND

Any land that is left to its own devices gradually becomes woodland again. But young woodland differs from ancient woodland. Most of the trees are ones that spread easily and grow fast, such as sycamores and birches. (Sycamore may also invade ancient woodlands, but will not be as widespread there.) If the wood is very new, there may still be plants typical of fields, such as cow parsley, beneath the trees. Ivy is also seen on the ground, whereas dog's mercury, which is common in old woods, will not be found. Some relatively young woods were planted, one or two centuries ago, as part of landscaped parklands. These often contain unexpected trees such as larch, copper beech or Scots pine.

Sycamore ▼
An Asian tree, probably introduced to Britain very early, perhaps by the Romans, and now found everywhere. Does well even on windy coasts.

▼ Silver birch
Tough but pretty trees that do well on sandy soils. They prefer the early stages of woodland formation, as scrub turns to forest.

Hazel ▼
As soon as the wood offers some shelter to wild animals they will set up home, bringing back hazelnuts and so introducing hazel to the wood.

Holly ▶
Birds perching in the young sycamore trees may have holly seeds in their droppings, and soon holly bushes are springing up below the trees.

Downy birch ▼
A tree that likes damp soil or even waterlogged conditions. Woods springing up on marshy ground often contain downy birch.

Ash ►
Found in ancient woodland, but also spreads to new woodland. Like sycamore, it has abundant wind-borne seeds that make it a good colonizer of wasteland.

Hawthorn ▼
Like holly, hawthorn is spread by birds. It springs up almost everywhere, and can be found in fields, hedgerows, scrub and ancient woods as well.

MATURE BEECH WOOD

Beech trees have roots that grab every drop of moisture around them, and they thrive on shallow, well-drained soils. On heavy, water-logged soils they cannot survive, while rich, deep soils are so good for oaks that the beech trees cannot compete. So beech woods are found mainly on chalk and limestone hillsides. Although beech woods may seem light and airy, they are actually short of light. Beech trees only let through 2% of the sunlight, and since they also monopolise the water in the soil, other plants are excluded. Planted beech woods, in particular, have a beautifully empty look, like huge cathedrals, often with no undergrowth, just a carpet of their own glossy brown leaves.

Downy birch ▶
On very poor, sandy, acid soils, downy birches may grow among the beeches.

Field maple ▼
This species can tolerate shade better than most trees, so it sometimes grows in the more open type of 'natural' beech wood.

Yew ▼
Yew bushes and small trees may grow beneath the beech trees, but their growth is stunted by the lack of light.

Beech
Stocky trees indicate natural woodland. Tall, slim, straight-trunked trees, close together, were probably planted for timber centuries ago.

◄ Ash
Naturally occurring beech-woods often contain other large trees, besides beech. The fast-growing ash is the most common of these.

Holly ▼
Enormous shade-tolerance makes holly an understorey shrub in some beech woods. An evergreen, with tough leaves, it needs little moisture.

PROJECT

The thick carpet of unrotted beech leaves is also a factor in stopping other plants from growing in beech woods. Find out exactly how long the leaves take to break down. Choose a quiet beechwood, mark the spot with a large stone, then put spots of red enamel paint onto 30 beech leaves surrounding the stone. Come back next year, and look for your leaves. Replace the newer leaves on top of them afterwards, and come back again the following year.

SCRUB

Scrub is a mixture of bushes, shrubs and small trees that grow on any abandoned farmland or garden. The scrub springs up once ploughing, grazing by sheep and cows, or lawn-mowing stops. Often the seeds of the shrubs and trees are in the soil already, or there are seedlings growing among the grass that have been stunted by grazing and are just waiting to grow. Unlike mature forest, scrub is a temporary state of affairs. With every year that passes the shrubs and trees get larger, and eventually their branch-tips meet to form a canopy. Once the ground is shaded, the grass dies back, followed by the less shade-tolerant shrubs. In time, scrub becomes young woodland.

Sallow ▼
The wind-borne seeds of willows and sallows arri early on, especially if th are large clumps of then growing somewhere nea

Elder ▼
Elderberries are popular with birds. Shrubs such as this only appear in scrubland once there are other small trees where birds can perch.

Blackthorn ▼
Blackthorn, or sloe, is spread to scrubland largely by badgers which eat the fruit and deposit the hard stones with their droppings.

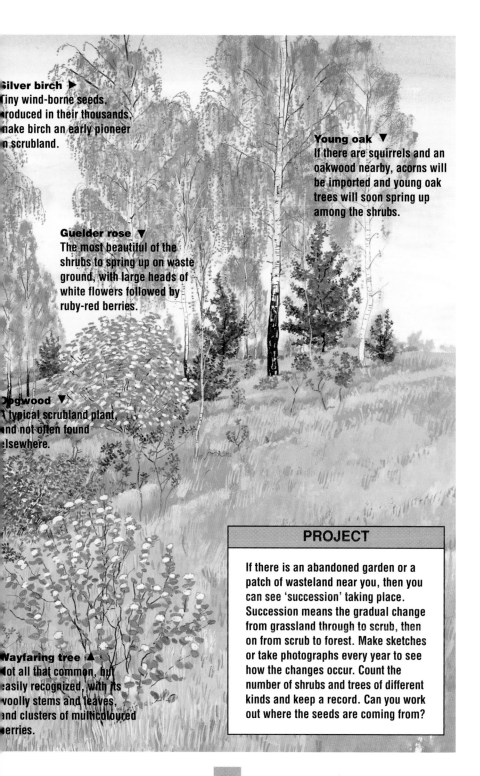

Silver birch ▶
Tiny wind-borne seeds, produced in their thousands, make birch an early pioneer in scrubland.

Young oak ▼
If there are squirrels and an oakwood nearby, acorns will be imported and young oak trees will soon spring up among the shrubs.

Guelder rose ▼
The most beautiful of the shrubs to spring up on waste ground, with large heads of white flowers followed by ruby-red berries.

Dogwood ▼
A typical scrubland plant, and not often found elsewhere.

Wayfaring tree ▲
Not all that common, but easily recognized, with its woolly stems and leaves, and clusters of multicoloured berries.

PROJECT

If there is an abandoned garden or a patch of wasteland near you, then you can see 'succession' taking place. Succession means the gradual change from grassland through to scrub, then on from scrub to forest. Make sketches or take photographs every year to see how the changes occur. Count the number of shrubs and trees of different kinds and keep a record. Can you work out where the seeds are coming from?

ANCIENT CONIFEROUS FOREST

Conifers are better than broadleaved trees at
withstanding very cold or very dry conditions.
For this reason, natural coniferous forests are
found mainly in the far north, particularly
Scandinavia. This is known as the boreal forest.
There are also natural coniferous forests in
central Europe where winters are very cold, on
high mountain slopes, and in the arid lands
around the Mediterranean. Some forests contain
both conifers and broadleaved trees, such as
those in southern Sweden and Norway. Unlike
the gloomy interior of a conifer plantation (see
p.38) a mature, natural coniferous forest has
open spaces in the canopy where light
penetrates, so there is far more undergrowth.

Birches ▼
Silver birch and downy birch
sometimes grow among the
conifers, creating a mixed
forest.

◄ Rowan
Rowan, or mountain ash,
may also grow among the
conifers, especially in
Scotland. The berries att
many birds.

Norway spruce ▼
The main conifer of the
boreal forest, along with
Scots pine. Like other
conifers, it tends to make the
soil acid with its fallen
needles.

◀ **Scots pine**
Can form forests of its own,
as in the Scottish highlands,
or be mixed with spruce. In
the long run, spruces usually
shade out the pines, except
on very poor gravelly soils.

PLANTATIONS

To produce wood quickly and cheaply, trees are planted close together in rows, with all the trees of the same species. A plantation such as this is, in some ways, more like a field of wheat than a forest. When conifers are planted in this way they let through very little light, and the interior of the plantation is dark and gloomy, with little or no undergrowth. As a result, there is not much bird or insect life. The main food resource of conifers – the nutritious seeds found inside the cones – are never produced by these young trees because they are felled too soon. Plantations could be made more useful to wildlife by planting the trees further apart, and using a mixture of different species.

Sitka spruce ▼
Used for cheap timber and paper-making. It comes from the west coast of North America, where there is plenty of rainfall, so it can survive in a wet climate.

◄ Douglas fir
Old timber plantations, where some of the trees have been cut down, look almost like real forests. These trees are often Douglas fir.

▼ Black Italian poplar
Grown for making matchsticks and rough wooden fruit boxes. Poplars form pretty little plantations that shimmer in the sunlight.

Norway spruce ▲
Grown in small plantations to supply Christmas trees. The trees are planted far apart to get a good shape.

FARMLAND

In times past, trees were a valuable part of a farm. Ash trees grew among the hedgerows, or at the edges of fields, and their branches were lopped occasionally to make the handles of farm tools. Beechnuts and sweet chestnuts were used for animal feed. Hazel was coppiced to supply small logs for the fire, and thin branches to weave into sheets of 'wattle' for the walls of houses. Oaks were kept for their timber, or for the shade they gave to the cattle on summer days. Today, trees are still used to shelter live-stock and as windbreaks, but most other uses have vanished. On some modern cereal farms there is not a tree to be seen, but many farmers keep some because they are part of the landscape.

Pollarded willow ▶
Along river banks, farmers grew pollarded willows. The slender stems that sprouted were used to weave baskets.

Pollarded oak ▶
Pollarded trees are cut back at intervals, much like coppiced trees, but higher up, so that cattle cannot eat the new shoots.

Hawthorn ▼
Used for hedging and shelter, but spreads at great speed unaided, thanks to the thorns that prevent animals from nibbling it back too much.

Ash
When under pressure, ash wood bends slightly but does not break as easily as other woods. This made it valuable for the handles of farm tools.

◀ **Field maple**
Sometimes used for hedging, and more rarely reaches tree size. The wood was once used to make bowls and other containers for food.

Wych elm ▲
Common in hedgerows where it is easily mistaken for hazel. Notice that the buds are brownish, not green, and the leaves almost stalkless.

SWAMPS AND MARSHES

Many trees have adapted to life in wet or water-logged soil, including aspen, alder and many of the willows. Once they are established in marshy areas, or in peat bogs, they change the land itself. By drawing water up from their roots to their leaves, the trees very gradually dry the soil out. Once it is drier, other trees can move in, and in time the whole area becomes an ordinary wood. This is another form of succession, like that seen in scrubland (p.34). Trees growing on waterlogged soil face many problems, including the difficulty of staying upright. The wet soil tends to move about their roots, and you will often see trees leaning drunkenly to one side.

Downy birch ▼
This species likes damp so
but will grow in drier place
as well. Like silver birch, i
is a good food source for
small birds.

◄ Aspen
Not usually in woods with
other trees, more often in
isolated damp spots in valley
bottoms, where the trees
grow very tall and slender.

Purple osier ►
Cultivated for its stems,
which are used in basket-
making, osier also grows
wild in marshy areas.

Ash ▼
The adaptable ash grows here, as well as in woods and hedges. On wet ground it is often small and shrubby with twisting stems.

Alder ▼
The native alder is almost entirely a wetland tree, favouring riversides and boggy patches in fields and woods.

Grey willow ▶
Tolerant of water about the roots, as are many willows. Larger willows do not often grow in marshes and bogs, but favour riversides.

REDWOODS

GIANT REDWOOD
Sequoiadendron
giganteum
Ll 0.4–1cm. Should have a
pointed top, but many are
struck by lightning, making
them rounded. Reaches 90m
in its native California; a few
reach 50m in Britain.

ORIGINS

The redwoods are a very old family of trees,
most of which died out millions of years ago.
The fourteen species that are left are found
mainly in China, Tasmania and on the west
coast of North America. These areas escaped the
worst of the cold weather during the Ice Ages,
so many trees and other plants survived here.

GENERAL FEATURES

These trees are grown in parks and large
gardens. Giant redwood and coast redwood
develop very long trunks, and are easy to spot
even at a distance. They have red felty bark that
comes off in threads – you can punch it hard
without hurting your fist. Swamp cypress and
dawn redwood lose their leaves in winter unlike
most conifers (cone-bearing trees).

Swamp cypresses come from
the famous swamps in the
bayou country of Louisiana
and other southern states in
the USA. Swamp water is
stagnant and low in oxygen,
so swamp cypresses push
special breathing roots up
above the ground.

JAPANESE RED CEDAR ▷
Cryptomeria japonica
Ll 0.6–1.5cm. A beautiful tree with glossy emerald green leaves. The bark peels off in strips.

COAST REDWOOD ◿
Sequoia sempervirens
Ll 0.6–2cm. Another tree from California, this species actually grows taller than the 'giant' redwood, reaching almost 120m. In Britain it only makes 40–50m.

SWAMP CYPRESS ▷
Taxodium distichum
Ll 0.8–2cm. If growing in wet ground, look out for the 'breathing roots'. The cones do not always have prickles.

◁ DAWN REDWOOD
Metasequoia glyptostroboides
Ll 1.2–6cm. Easily told from swamp cypress by the fact that the side shoots grow out in pairs from the same point on the main stem, not alternately.

CYPRESSES

MONTEREY CYPRESS
Cupressus macrocarpa
Ll 1–2mm. A true cypress.
Smell is the best way to
identify this species.
Crush a leaf and it will
smell of lemons.

GENERAL FEATURES

Cypresses and their relatives (the junipers and
thujas) have an unusual characteristic – they
have one type of leaf when young and another
when they get older. The young leaves are spiky
needles, the adult ones are tiny 'scales' that lie
flat on the stem. Some ornamental cypresses
have young leaves even when grown up.

TWO KINDS OF CYPRESS

There are two kinds of cypress, called the true
cypresses and false cypresses. Don't be misled by
these names – both really are cypresses! If you
hold out the frond of a false cypress, and look at
it from the side, it will be more or less flat, like
the leaf of a fern. Fronds of true cypress are not
flat, because the stems branch in all directions.

Hybrids
A number of the trees you
see in parks and gardens are
hybrids. These are produced
by crossing two different
species, or, in the highly
unusual case of the Leyland
cypress, two species from
different genera. Like the
mule, which is a cross
between a horse and a
donkey, the Leyland cypress
is very vigorous but cannot
produce offspring.

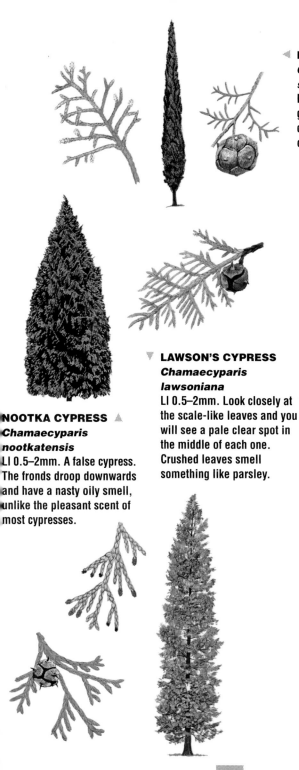

ITALIAN CYPRESS
Cupressus sempervirens
LI 0.5–1mm. The branches grow straight up giving it a candle-like shape. Usually only grown in gardens.

LAWSON'S CYPRESS
Chamaecyparis lawsoniana
LI 0.5–2mm. Look closely at the scale-like leaves and you will see a pale clear spot in the middle of each one. Crushed leaves smell something like parsley.

NOOTKA CYPRESS
Chamaecyparis nootkatensis
LI 0.5–2mm. A false cypress. The fronds droop downwards and have a nasty oily smell, unlike the pleasant scent of most cypresses.

LEYLAND CYPRESS
X Cupressocyparis leylandii
LI 0.5–2mm. Produced by plant breeders who crossed a false cypress with a true cypress. It rarely produces cones, but grows at a frantic pace instead.

THUJAS AND JUNIPERS

GENERAL FEATURES

All these trees are members of the cypress family. Thujas, such as the western red cedar, are larger than most cypresses and have beautiful glossy foliage. Incense cedar comes from North America. Just to confuse matters, pencil cedar is actually a type of juniper!

CONES LIKE BERRIES

Junipers are a very strange type of conifer. Their cones have evolved into fleshy, blue-skinned structures that look just like berries. (Berries, of course, are fruits, and these are only found on flowering trees and plants, not on conifers.) Juniper leaves are also odd. Like cypresses, they have two different kinds of leaves (see p.46), but many junipers never grow any adult leaves.

Juniper 'berries' are not real berries but modified cones. They have a woody, aromatic taste and are sometimes used to flavour meat. In the wild, they are eaten by birds.

COMMON JUNIPER
Juniperus communis
Ll 0.8–2cm. A native shrub although it is only found growing in a few places on chalky soil. Rabbits eat young juniper plants, and this keeps numbers down.

PENCIL CEDAR
Juniperus virginiana
Ll 0.5–1.5mm. This juniper
has both adult leaves
(scales) and juvenile leaves
(spiky needles). Both may be
found growing from the same
stem.

WESTERN RED CEDAR
Thuja plicata
Ll 2–3mm. Its leaves have a
strong pineapple scent. Used
by American Indians to make
dug-out canoes and totem
poles.

CHINESE JUNIPER
Juniperus chinensis
Ll 1.5mm. This species has
both adult and juvenile leaves.
Look inside the canopy to
see the juvenile leaves.

PROJECT

In spring, look out for the young cones
of these trees. They are tiny and not like
cones at all. They appear at the tips of
the shoots, and some are bright yellow,
orange or pink. Watch them through the
year: the females will slowly develop
into woody cones, or into juniper
berries. The males will shed their
pollen and then fall off. Draw or paint
each stage so you can compare them
and see how they change.

INCENSE CEDAR
Calocedrus decurrens
Ll 0.5–3mm. A striking tree
whose rounded top
distinguishes it from others
with this candle-like shape.
An American species seen in
gardens in Europe.

TRUE CEDARS AND LARCHES

ATLAS CEDAR
Cedrus atlantica
Ll 1–3cm. This tree comes from the Atlas mountains in North Africa. It is recognized by the young twigs which bend upwards at the ends.

GENERAL FEATURES

True cedars and larches produce their leaves in little bunches, like tufts of short hair. One important difference is that larches drop their leaves in winter, whereas cedars (like most other conifers) do not. Cedar cones are much larger than larch cones – they look like big wooden eggs – and the trees have statuesque shapes. Larches are often very spindly and wind-blown by comparison, with small lightweight cones.

CHARACTERISTICS

Because they grow new leaves each year, larches have quite soft foliage. In winter, you can recognize them by their rough-barked twigs, which have little cylindrical knobs all along them, where the bunches of leaves grew out.

Larches are forest trees, and wind-speeds are always less in a forest, the trees protecting each other from the full force of the gale. So larches are not well-suited to growing in unsheltered sites, where they develop lop-sided shapes.

DEODAR
Cedrus deodara
Ll 2–5cm. The young twigs hang down at the tips, unlike Atlas cedar. This species comes from the Himalayan mountains.

CEDAR OF LEBANON ▷
Cedrus libani
Ll 2–3cm. Few are left in Lebanon itself, but these magnificent trees, with their unmistakable stately shape, are widely planted in parks.

JAPANESE LARCH
Larix kaempferi
Ll 1.5–3cm. Difficult to tell apart from common larch, but the twigs are darker, purplish, orange, or reddish, and the leaves paler.

COMMON LARCH ▲
Larix decidua
Ll 1–3cm. A tree from the high mountains of Europe, grown here for ornament, timber and sometimes for shelter. Needles turn golden brown before they fall.

SILVER FIRS

COMMON SILVER FIR
Abies alba
Ll 1.5–3cm. An introduced tree, like all those shown here. Look for two narrow white bands under each leaf, and grey-brown twigs with a few darker hairs.

GENERAL FEATURES

There are two types of trees called firs – silver firs and Douglas firs – and they are not all that closely related. Both types can easily be confused with spruces and hemlocks, and some tips for distinguishing them are given on p.54.

LOOKING AT CONES

You will be lucky to get a silver fir cone because they only grow at the tops of the trees, and they break up on the tree instead of falling to the ground intact. But it is worth craning your neck to see the cones. Although they are long and cylindrical, as spruce cones are, they stand *upright* from the branches rather than hanging downwards. Douglas fir cones hang down, and have very long bracts (or scales) sticking out between the normal cone scales.

Like many conifers, firs produce resin whenever the bark, trunk or branches are damaged. The resin smells pleasant to us but not to insects, and it helps to deter them from feeding on the tree. Here resin drips from the cut branch of a fir.

NOBLE FIR
Abies procera
LI 1–3.5cm. A silver fir with two dull greyish bands under each leaf. The twigs are much more reddish-brown than in common silver fir, with fine reddish hairs.

GRAND FIR ▲
Abies grandis
LI 2–6cm. A silver fir, planted widely for timber. Large glossy leaves, with two silvery bands below, that smell of marmalade when they are crushed.

DOUGLAS FIR
Pseudotsuga menziesii
LI 2–3.5cm. The soft leaves smell fruity. It is named after the Scottish botanist, David Douglas, who discovered it in America.

CAUCASIAN FIR ▶
Abies nordmanniana
LI 1.5–3.5cm. A silver fir with two bold white bands under the leaf. The leaves are a darker and glossier green than common silver fir.

HEMLOCKS AND SPRUCES

GENERAL FEATURES OF CONES

Spruce cones are very distinctive: long, smooth in outline and flexible (you can bend them in your hands without them snapping). They hang downwards from the branches and can often be found lying on the ground beneath the trees. Hemlock cones are almost like miniature versions of these, often less than 2cm long, although there is one species, the mountain hemlock, which has cones up to 7cm long.

HABITAT

Like the silver firs and Douglas firs, none of these trees are native. You will see them only where they have been planted, and this is mainly in plantations and botanic gardens.

To most people, hemlock means poison, but the poisonous hemlock is a European hedgerow plant not a tree. The first hemlock tree known to Europeans was eastern hemlock, whose crushed leaves smell similar to the poisonous hemlock.

NORWAY SPRUCE
Picea abies
Ll 1–2.5cm. To remember how the leaves of spruces feel, think of fitting the decorations on a Christmas tree! The Norway spruce has been used for this purpose for 150 years.

BREWER'S WEEPING ▷ SPRUCE
Picea breweriana
Ll 2.5–3cm. Called 'weeping' because the side shoots hang downwards, but this is a wild tree, not a cultivated variety like the weeping willow or weeping ash.

WESTERN HEMLOCK ◢
Tsuga heterophylla
Ll 0.6–2cm. You can recognize hemlocks at a distance because the tops tend to droop. The twigs of this hemlock are covered by long cream-coloured hairs.

◁ SITKA SPRUCE
Picea sitchensis
Ll 15–30cm. This is the tree seen growing in large blocks on hillsides and moorlands. The leaves are a blue-green colour, with white stripes underneath.

HOW TO IDENTIFY

Silver firs (a), spruces (b), hemlocks (c) and Douglas firs (d) all look alike. To identify them, inspect the leaves and twigs. Silver fir leaves have tiny 'suckers' at the base and where they fall off they leave a flat, circular scar. Douglas fir leaves have a short stalk, and leave an oval bump on the twig. Spruces and hemlocks have woody stumps at the base of each leaf, which are left behind when the leaves fall. Spruce leaves are harsh and often spiky, while hemlock leaves are soft.

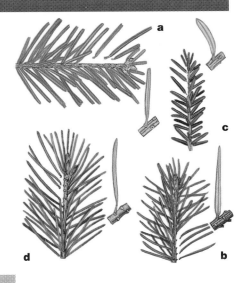

PINES

SCOTS PINE
Pinus sylvestris
Ll 2.5–8cm. This tree is native to northern and central Europe. The reddish flaking bark near the top of the trunk is distinctive.

COUNTING THE NEEDLES

Pines are distinguished by their very long needles. These are produced in bundles, with two, three or five needles per bundle. The number of needles in a bundle is important for identification: all the species here have two.

GENERAL FEATURES

Apart from their long needles, pine trees have distinctive cones. These are hard and woody, with a knob at the centre (or sometimes the tip) of each scale. Pine cones can open and close their scales as the humidity of the air changes, to control the spread of pollen or seeds. The neat conical shape of most conifers is seen in young pines, but mature pines often have very interesting, irregular shapes.

Pines are usually thought of as cold-climate trees, but some of those grown for ornament in Britain, such as the maritime pine, actually come from the shores of the Mediterranean.

AUSTRIAN PINE ▽
Pinus nigra* var. *nigra
Ll 10–15cm. This is a very variable species. Some trees have such dark leaves that they seem to be blackened by soot.

MOUNTAIN PINE ▲
Pinus uncinata
Ll 3–8cm. The stiff, dense needles of this pine seem to spiral around the shoots. The bark is greyish-pink but can turn almost black.

MARITIME PINE ▽
Pinus pinaster
Ll 10–25cm. This pine has long, hard, sharp-pointed needles, and a small prickle on each scale of the cone.

SHORE PINE ▽
Pinus contorta* var. *contorta
Ll 3–7cm. This tree is sometimes seen in timber plantations. The needles are packed together very densely on the stems. Both needles and shoots may be twisted.

PINES

MONTEREY PINE
Pinus radiata
Ll 10–15cm. Often grown as an ornamental tree near the sea, as it can withstand dry winds. The large, lop-sided cones may stay on the tree for years.

GENERAL FEATURES

Shown here are the three-needled and five-needled pines (see p. 56). These are often very attractive trees, so they are planted in parks and gardens. The needles are very long in some species, and a few have crinkly or bent needles.

TREES OF MONTEREY

Monterey pine is found only in the Monterey peninsula. It grows gnarled and stunted in Monterey, but gets much larger when planted in cooler climates, showing that it is not ideally suited to Monterey. During the Ice Ages, cold-loving conifer forests 'moved' south by seeding themselves. As the Ice Ages ended the forests slowly 'moved' north again. But Monterey was then an island, and the trees there could not go north, nor be ousted by others coming in from the south.

Pines are often attacked by the caterpillars of the pine beauty moth, especially pines in large plantations. Look closely for the caterpillars, which have green-and-white striped bodies, making them very well camouflaged against the pine needles.

AROLLA PINE
Pinus cembra
Ll 5–8cm. Pull the needles outwards and you will see a brilliant bluish-white inner surface. The cones are unusual, like globe artichokes.

WEYMOUTH PINE
Pinus strobus
Ll 5–14cm. Also known as white pine. Bluish-green needles and long slender cones that hang downwards, almost like spruce cones, identify this species.

PROJECT

Make a collection of cones from all the different pine trees you see. You can usually find some cones lying on the ground. Collect a few needles as well, and label all your finds with the date and place. Remember to make a note of the tree's shape and size as well. When you have samples from ten or more trees, then you can compare them and try to identify the individual species.

BHUTAN PINE
Pinus wallichiana
Ll 8–20cm. The slender, elegant needles of this pine can reach up to 20cm in length. They make this a very attractive tree for parks and gardens.

PALMS AND OTHERS

A LIVING FOSSIL

All the trees shown here are misfits. The strangest is the ginkgo, or maidenhair, a 'living fossil' found only in a tiny area of China. Others of its kind became extinct over 100 million years ago. The ginkgo is more closely related to conifers than to flowering trees.

UNUSUAL TREES

None of the other trees here are as odd as the ginkgo. Yew and monkey puzzle are both unusual types of conifer. The palm trees belong to a group of plants called the 'monocotyledons' which all have leaves with parallel veins. They include the grasses, irises and lilies. Palms are the only real trees in this group. Because grass-like plants grow differently from other flowering plants, palm trees cannot form proper trunks. The trunk is built up from the bases of dead leaves and cannot grow fatter as the tree gets older.

Yew trees are often the first to show signs of damage by acid rain. Some needles fall off leaving others in clumps – sometimes called the 'tinsel effect'. The needles also turn a tawny yellow. Severe frost, drought and disease can produce the same symptoms.

YEW
Taxus baccata
Ll 1–4cm. A native tree, often planted in churchyards. The soft, dark leaves on a green stem resemble *Sequoia*, but have no scent.

GINKGO ▷
Ginkgo biloba
LI 5–10cm. Notice the primitive leaves, with no midrib, and simple unbranched veins all radiating from the leaf-stalk.

MONKEY PUZZLE ▽
Araucaria araucaria
LI 3–4cm. Unmistakable tree shape. One of a group of unusual conifers found in parks and gardens.

EUROPEAN FAN PALM ▽
Chamaerops humilis
LI 50–80cm. No more than 3m tall. The only palm native to Europe, it is found on sandy soils in Mediterranean countries.

CHUSAN PALM ◁
Trachycarpus fortunei
LI 50–80cm. Also known as Chinese Windmill palm. A fairly hardy palm, used to life in the mountains of southern China, and grown for ornament in Europe.

CABBAGE PALM △
Cordyline australis
LI 30–90cm. Not a palm tree at all, but an agave, related to the yuccas that are sometimes grown as houseplants. From New Zealand, but widely planted in Europe.

WILLOWS

CRACK WILLOW
Salix fragilis
Ll 6–15cm. On river banks, look for bright red roots sticking out into the water. Those of white willow are yellowish-white.

HABITAT

Willows are mainly trees of damp places, such as riversides and swampy ground. But most will grow in dry ground as well, as long as they are not competing with other trees, so you may see weeping willows (see p.64) in parks or gardens. Pussy willow, in particular, can do without wet soil, and often grows in hedgerows.

USEFUL TREES

Willows have been used for centuries to make baskets, chairs and other furniture. The main species used is osier. It is grown in flooded beds, and cut back to the base every year. Long, straight, narrow stems sprout up from the stump, and these are cut to make willow wands. When wet, the wands bend and can be woven into baskets.

Pollarded willows are cut back to the stump every 2–5 years. Those in the distance have recently been cut back and are left with just the trunk. Those in the foreground were cut back several years ago, and have now produced a thick crop of shoots – called 'willow wands'.

WHITE WILLOW ▷

Salix alba

.l 5–10cm. Difficult to tell
from crack willow, but small
twigs branch off from the
main twig at a narrow angle
– those of crack willow stick
out sharply.

PUSSY WILLOW ▽

Salix caprea

.l 6–11cm. Also known as
goat willow. There are other
small willows that are
sometimes called pussy
willow, but this is the main
one. Look for a dark red,
hairy leaf-stalk.

OSIER ▽

Salix viminalis

.l 10–25cm. Extremely long
narrow leaves mark this
willow out. Not often seen in
the wild, except where it was
once grown for basket-
making.

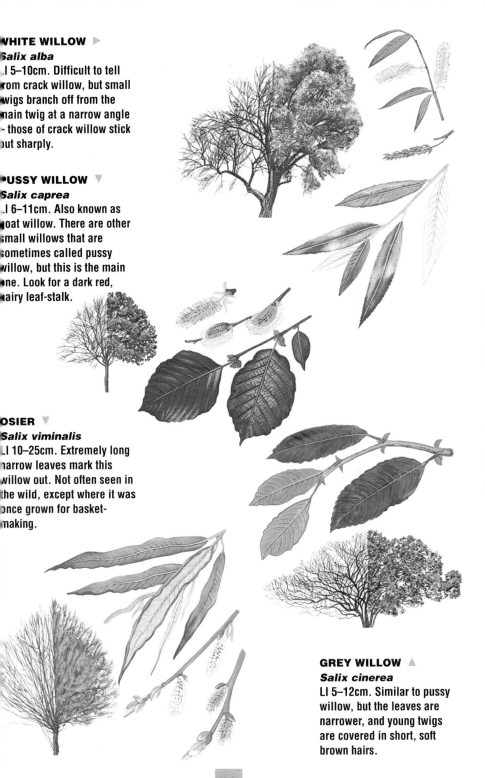

GREY WILLOW ▲

Salix cinerea

Ll 5–12cm. Similar to pussy
willow, but the leaves are
narrower, and young twigs
are covered in short, soft
brown hairs.

WILLOWS

WEEPING WILLOW
Salix X chrysocoma
LI 10–15cm. The only similar tree is Chinese weeping willow which has brown, not golden, twigs.

TREES WITH CATKINS

Willows have tiny flowers packed together in catkins. These usually hang downwards and shake in the breeze, making the flowers release pollen. For trees that are wind-pollinated, the catkin is a cunning device for scattering pollen only when the wind is blowing. The earliest flowers were insect-pollinated, and wind pollinated species evolved from these.

ORNAMENTAL VARIETIES

There are many ornamental varieties of willow, produced by breeding and selection. In the case of weeping willow, white willow was crossed with a Chinese willow with 'weeping' branches. The hybrid produced is much stronger than the Chinese weeping willow. Contorted willows appeared suddenly due to a mutation, or genetic change, in the seed of a Japanese willow.

One type of willow is grown solely for making cricket bats. Called cricket-bat willow, it grows very fast, reaching 20m in 15 years. The trunk is cut into logs of bat length, then split lengthwise with a wedge and mallet. The triangular segments produced are then carved into bats.

CONTORTED WILLOW ▽
Salix matsudana 'Tortuosa'
Ll 6–8cm. Unmistakable – a tree that looks as if it has been wearing curlers. Notice that the twigs and branches are also twisted.

BAY WILLOW ▲
Salix pentandra
Ll 5–12cm. A rare tree, but native to parts of Europe. The dark, glossy leaves have a rich scent when crushed, like bay leaves.

PROJECT

Growing willows is very easy. Snap off a few twigs and push them into soil in a pot. Soon there will be roots growing from the bottom and leaves from the top of each twig. Willows have this unusual talent because it is helpful for them in spreading along rivers. If twigs are snapped off by the wind they float downstream and can take root wherever they come to rest.

VIOLET WILLOW ▽
Salix daphnoides
Ll 5–10cm. 'Violet' is an exaggeration – the twigs are a dull purple. This is a wild species grown for ornament.

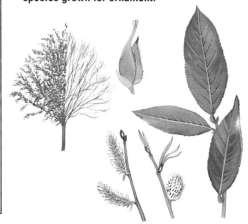

POPLARS

NOISY TREES

Identifying trees with your eyes shut is not easy, but there are two trees shown here that you *could* pick out blindfolded. One is the aspen, whose leaves have long flexible stalks and tremble in the slightest breeze. This makes a loud rustling noise that is unmistakable if you have heard it once. Other poplars also shake and shimmer in the breeze, but none makes such a loud noise as the aspen.

SCENTED TREES

Balsam poplars can be identified by their rich smell, which is like old-fashioned ointment. This comes from the sticky coating of the buds but it often scents the air all around. The only other trees to have such a strong perfume are limes, which are very fragrant when in flower.

Why so hairy?
The thick layer of white felt underneath a white poplar leaf must be there for a reason, but no one knows exactly why. The only other tree with leaves this hairy is whitebeam, which grows on dry hillsides; the felt is thought to reduce water loss from its leaves. Unlike whitebeam, poplars typically grow in damp soil. Perhaps the hairs help to keep off leaf-eating insects. The fact that hair also covers the buds and young twigs make this a plausible explanation.

WHITE POPLAR
Populus alba
Ll 6–12cm. No other tree has such bright white undersides to the leaves. The leaf shape varies – some are rounded, like grey poplar, others more maple-like.

ASPEN ▲
Populus tremula
Ll 3–8cm. Likes damp places, and is not very common. Unlike grey poplar, it has hairless twigs, and leaves without a felty layer underneath.

BALSAM POPLARS ▲
Populus balsamifera, Populus trichocarpa and hybrids
Ll 5–10cm. Sniff the buds rather than looking too hard at the leaf shape – this varies quite a bit.

GREY POPLAR ▲
Populus canescens
Ll 5–8cm. The greyish felt under the leaves is lost by autumn, unlike white poplar. The leaves are nearly always rounded in shape.

PROJECT

♂

♀

In early spring, look out for poplar catkins. (They appear before the leaves so it will help if you know where to find poplars in advance.) Most poplar trees are either male or female – try to work out which sex yours are. The male catkins have small, red knob-like anthers (male part of the flower). You can check if you were right later in the summer – male catkins will all have fallen off, but the females should have developed into seeds.

POPLARS

BLACK POPLAR
Populus nigra
Ll 5–10cm. A much smaller, more gnarled and slower growing tree than the hybrid black poplars.

GENERAL FEATURES

All these trees are very similar, apart from the Lombardy poplar. The true black poplar is a native tree, but an uncommon one. It prefers marshy ground. The rough trunk and branches, covered with bumps, and bristling with young shoots, are its most striking feature. By contrast, the hybrid black poplars have a long, clean trunk, sweeping upwards.

HUNDREDS OF HYBRIDS

North American poplars are known as cottonwoods because of their fluffy white seeds. Almost 300 years ago, seeds of a cottonwood were brought from America and when the trees grew and flowered they were crossed (hybridised) with European black poplar. This cross, and others, produced the hybrid black poplars.

Lombardy poplars are often planted in towns – sometimes with terrible results. Their thirsty, vigorous roots soak up all the water around them. On clay soil this can cause shrinkage and movement, producing cracks in buildings nearby as their foundations move.

HYBRID BLACK ▽ POPLARS

Populus X 'Serotina'
(illustrated), *Populus X* 'Regenerata' and others
LI 8–12cm. Notice the straight trunk, tapering to a main branch that often grows off to one side near the top of the tree.

LOMBARDY POPLAR △

Populus nigra 'Italica'
LI 5–8cm. A tree that everyone knows, bred in Italy in 1758 from the native black poplar. Only the male trees grow into the typical shape; the females are upswept but not as neat.

BALM OF GILEAD △

Populus X candicans
LI 5–10cm. Another hybrid, with strong reddish-brown stems and large yellowish leaves. It has some of the scent of a balsam poplar, but is not as strong.

HOW TO WATCH

To find out how fast the fastest trees grow, organize a tree race. Look round parks and roadsides then ask your friends to each choose a tree. Look for young trees and choose vigorous species: hybrid black poplars, grey or white poplars, balsam poplars, Balm of Gilead, sycamores, eucalyptuses or Leyland cypresses (make sure these will be allowed to grow into trees and not cut back to hedge height). Measure the heights twice a year (p.15 tells you how).

WALNUT, FIG AND MULBERRY

WALNUT
Juglans regia
Ll 6–15cm. When crushed, leaves produce a brown liquid and have a strange, unpleasant, smell. In spring, the leaves are bright red at first – only 'tree-of-heaven' shares this colour.

HABITATS

The fig and the mulberry are pioneers. They belong to a family of plants that grow widely in the tropics, but not elsewhere. Like all plants and animals, this family includes a few species that have spread to the edges of their natural region, and a little way beyond: natural pioneers. Most figs grow in tropical rainforests where they clamber up the huge trees and provide a feast of fruit for parrots and monkeys. The fig we know grows naturally in Asia, and was brought to Europe by the Romans.

UNUSUAL BUDS

Walnuts are unusual in having two kinds of bud, one which contains the leaves and another for the catkins. The hickories, which belong to the same family (along with pecan nuts, which we eat) have their own unusual feature. They bear their catkins in threes, branching from a single stalk.

Silk is produced from the coccoons of certain moths. The caterpillars which spin these valuable coccoons are known as silkworms, and like to feed on the leaves of the white mulberry tree. White mulberry only grows well in warmer climates, but silk production is practised in the south of France.

SHAGBARK HICKORY
Carya alba
Ll 10–20cm. Seen mainly in botanic gardens in Britain and Europe. Notice the unusual leaf-shape.

BLACK MULBERRY
Morus nigra
Ll 6–20cm. Unmistakable when in fruit, but notice that limes and some poplars also have heart-shaped leaves. An oriental tree whose fruits are a major part of the diet in Afghanistan.

BLACK WALNUT
Juglans nigra
Ll 6–12cm. An American introduced tree. It has more leaflets per leaf than the common walnut, usually about 15.

FIG
Ficus carica
Ll 10–20cm. Only seen in Southern Britain as it likes warm conditions. Fruits are eaten fresh or dried.

BIRCHES AND ALDERS

GENERAL FEATURES

All these trees belong to the same family. They have their flowers packed together in catkins and are pollinated by the wind. None grow very tall – they are the sort of trees that spring up quickly from seed, grow fast, and die without ever getting huge and gnarled. But in their short lives they produce a lot of seeds, so there are plenty of young trees following on behind them. Such trees are known as 'opportunists' and they do well on scrubland (silver birches), marshy places (downy birch) or by rivers (alder).

NON-CONIFEROUS CONES

Alders are flowering plants, so they produce true fruits around their seeds. But their fruits have evolved to be hard and woody – so they look, superficially, like cones! These woody cones suit the alder because its seeds fall out into the water and float downstream.

Birches growing on a bog in Wales. By rights, these should be downy birches, but notice the bright white trunks. They are natural hybrids between silver birch and downy birch, with the silvery trunks of one and the water tolerance of the other.

SILVER BIRCH
Betula pendula
Ll 2–7cm. Well known for its silvery trunk. Watch out for hybrids between this species and downy birch – they cross with each other naturally.

72

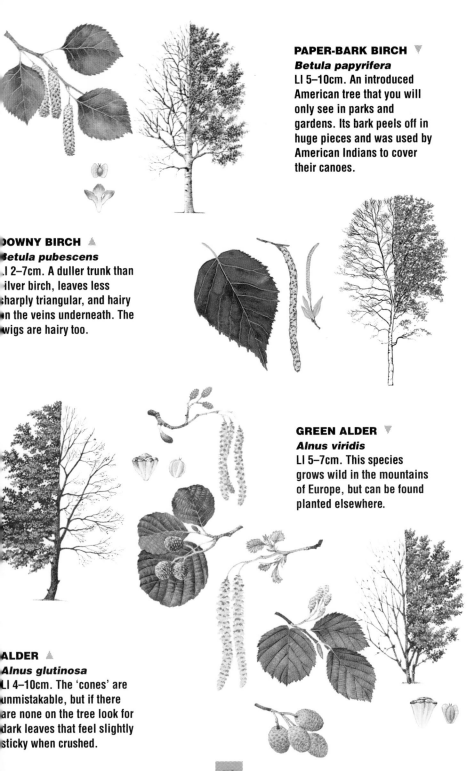

PAPER-BARK BIRCH ▽
Betula papyrifera
Ll 5–10cm. An introduced American tree that you will only see in parks and gardens. Its bark peels off in huge pieces and was used by American Indians to cover their canoes.

DOWNY BIRCH ▲
Betula pubescens
Ll 2–7cm. A duller trunk than silver birch, leaves less sharply triangular, and hairy on the veins underneath. The twigs are hairy too.

GREEN ALDER ▽
Alnus viridis
Ll 5–7cm. This species grows wild in the mountains of Europe, but can be found planted elsewhere.

ALDER ▲
Alnus glutinosa
Ll 4–10cm. The 'cones' are unmistakable, but if there are none on the tree look for dark leaves that feel slightly sticky when crushed.

ELMS AND HAZEL

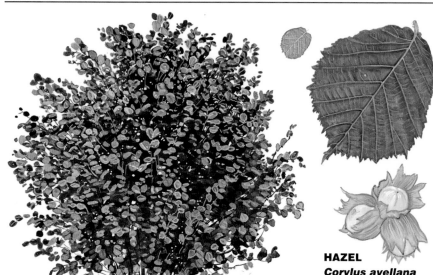

IDENTIFICATION

Elms and hazel are unrelated, but their leaves are easily confused, especially when growing in hedgerows, where there are no other clues to look for. With hazel, remember that its leaves vary enormously in shape and size – some are as big and round as saucers, while others are as small as the bowl of a teaspoon. But they usually have a covering of rough reddish-coloured hairs, and longish leaf-stalks. They are also symmetrical at the base, while elm leaves generally have a lobe on one side of the stalk. The buds of hazel are green, not brown.

PLENTIFUL NUTS

Hazels produce huge numbers of nuts in the autumn, which are eaten by mice, voles, jays and woodpeckers. Look on the ground below hazel trees or bushes and you will see shells that have been nibbled open.

HAZEL
Corylus avellana
Ll 3–15cm. Very common in hedgerows and in woods, usually growing under other trees. Often coppiced in the past. Nuts often eaten by squirrels and mice.

Hazel has the unusual habit of developing its catkins six or seven months before they are needed. When the leaves fall in the autumn, next year's catkin's are already well developed. This allows hazel to flower very early, often in February.

74

FILBERT
Corylus maxima
Ll 4–16cm. Related to the hazel. A Mediterranean species that is grown commercially for its nuts.

WYCH ELM
Ulmus glabra
Ll 10–18cm. A native tree, and quite common. The leaves are hairy beneath and rough on top, with almost no stalk. Does not produce many shoots, unlike most elms, but has huge bunches of seeds in autumn.

ENGLISH ELM
Ulmus procera
Ll 6–10cm. Now rare due to Dutch elm disease. Young trees spring up everywhere but soon die. Look for 'herringbone' twigs and corky bark on the branches.

SMOOTH-LEAVED ELM
Ulmus minor
Ll 6–10cm. Leaves usually smooth above with a few hairs below, and a short (5mm) stalk. There are many varieties of this tree.

BEECH, HORNBEAM & CHESTNUT

BEECH
Fagus sylvatica
Ll 4–10cm. Beech trees always have a thick carpet of small, prickly beech nut shells and glossy brown leaves around them, so they are easy to recognize, even in winter.

IDENTIFICATION

Beech and hornbeam are shown together here because they can easily be confused. Hornbeam belongs to the birch, alder and hazel family, while beech and sweet chestnut belong with the oaks. Notice that beech leaves are remarkably smooth and silky, with a wavy margin, whereas hornbeam leaves have tiny teeth around the edge. The brown buds of beech are long and sharply pointed, while hornbeam buds are smaller and usually chequered brown and green.

GROWN FOR THEIR WOOD

Sweet chestnut was brought to Britain by the Romans, and is still grown for fencing timber. Beech was once widely planted for furniture-making, and many of these beautiful beech woods remain. Hornbeam wood is extremely hard and was made into cogs for windmills. Today, it is used for butchers' blocks.

Beeches are often used for 'laid hedges', in which the supple trunks of the saplings are bent sideways and woven together. If the hedge is later abandoned, the beeches may grow into proper trees, but with a bend still in the trunk.

SWEET CHESTNUT ▲
Castanea sativa
Ll 10–25cm. Very long leaves make this tree unmistakable. In winter, look at the bark: it spirals around the trunk like a helter-skelter.

HORNBEAM
Carpinus betulus
Ll 4–10cm. Look for the distinctive seeds and chequered buds. The trunk usually has many ridges running up it, and may twist or bend.

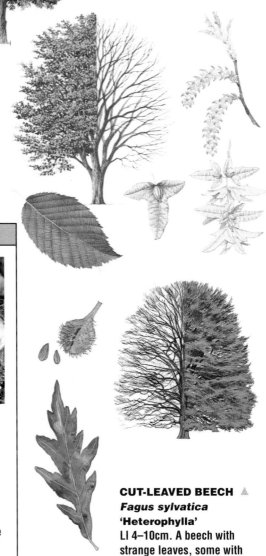

PROJECT

Beech nuts are known as 'mast' and were once very important as food for pigs. Take the two nuts out of their prickly case, and bite open the shiny brown skin to see what they taste like. Chestnuts have more flesh and are much better to eat. Collect them when they fall and roast them over a fire or barbecue, or in an oven. Break open the outer skin and eat the nuts inside.

CUT-LEAVED BEECH ▲
Fagus sylvatica
'Heterophylla'
Ll 4–10cm. A beech with strange leaves, some with 'frayed' edges, others lobed.

OAKS

TREES OF LEGEND

If you ask most people to think of a tree they will think of an oak. Oaks, especially common oaks, can live for up to 800 years. They feature in many legends and fairy stories, and King Charles I was supposed to have hidden from the Roundheads in an oak tree, which is why many pubs are called "The Royal Oak". The oak leaf and acorn are used as symbols for all sorts of different purposes.

USEFUL TREES

The common oak is a spreading tree with massive curved branches. When ships were built of wood, the curved timber from these branches was the only thing that could be used for the ships' hulls. The navy depended on a constant supply of these old oaks, and there were laws protecting them.

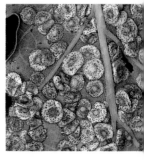

Oaks play host to an enormous number of insect species, and many form galls on different parts of the tree. The gall is a protective layer within which the insect larva feeds and grows, safe from most predators. Galls develop because the insect interferes with the plant's normal pattern of growth. The galls shown here are oak spangle galls.

COMMON OAK
Quercus robur
LI 10–12cm. Also called 'pedunculate oak' for the dangling acorns. These are often replaced by knobbly diamond-shaped galls, the work of a gall wasp.

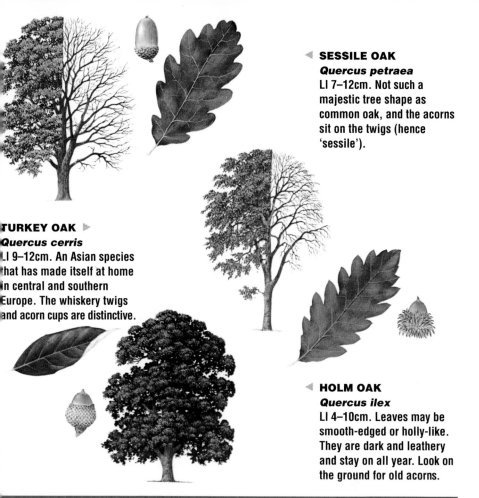

SESSILE OAK
Quercus petraea
Ll 7–12cm. Not such a majestic tree shape as common oak, and the acorns sit on the twigs (hence 'sessile').

TURKEY OAK ▷
Quercus cerris
Ll 9–12cm. An Asian species that has made itself at home in central and southern Europe. The whiskery twigs and acorn cups are distinctive.

HOLM OAK
Quercus ilex
Ll 4–10cm. Leaves may be smooth-edged or holly-like. They are dark and leathery and stay on all year. Look on the ground for old acorns.

HOW TO IDENTIFY

These oaks are the most common. Holm oak is only grown in parks and gardens. The other three grow in woods and farmland but Turkey oak is uncommon: look for woody 'whiskers' on the twigs and rub the leaves which feel like fine sandpaper. If it is not a Turkey oak, then look at the leaf stalks and acorns. Acorns on a long stem and almost stalkless leaves identify common oak. Acorns sitting on the twigs and stalked leaves indicate sessile oak.

OAKS

GENERAL FEATURES

Acorns are the trademark of oak trees everywhere, and make mature trees easy to spot in the autumn. Most oaks also have the characteristic oak leaves but some oaks do have simpler leaves, especially evergreens such as the holm oak and cork oak. None of the species here develops the heavy twisted branches of the common oak.

HABITAT

Downy oak and cork oak are both European trees. The cork oak has been cultivated for thousands of years because its thick bark can be cut off and made into the cork stoppers of wine bottles, as well as cork flooring and fishing floats. Red oak, scarlet oak and pin oak, however, are all American trees that are rarely seen outside arboreta and large gardens.

In France and other European countries, oaks are associated with truffles, round black fungi, as prized by gourmets as caviar or oysters. The truffles grow mainly under oaks, but only in relatively undisturbed woods. Trained dogs or pigs are used to sniff them out. Truffles do grow in Britain, but are now rare.

DOWNY OAK
Quercus pubescens
LI 4–13cm. The most common oak in the south of France and other parts of southern and western Europe, but rare in Britain. Look for the soft, dense hairs on the young twigs and leaf stalks.

RED OAK ▲
Quercus rubra
LI 12–22cm. Named for its autumn colours, although these do not develop as well in Europe as in its native land, North America.

SCARLET OAK
Quercus coccinea
LI 7–15cm. Another North American oak, not as common as red oak, and generally smaller. This species, too, is noted for its autumn colour which is often better in Europe than that of red oak.

PIN OAK ▶
Quercus palustris
LI 12–22cm. Notice the spiky tips to the leaf lobes which are shared with other North American oaks belonging to this group, red oak and scarlet oak.

UNUSUAL FLOWERING TREES

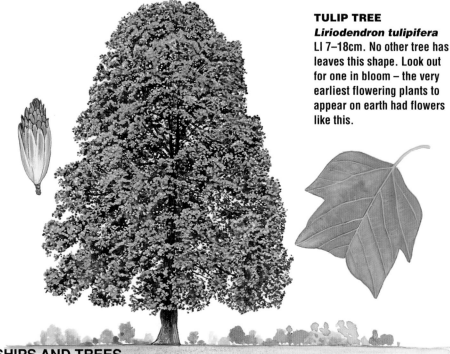

TULIP TREE
Liriodendron tulipifera
LI 7–18cm. No other tree has leaves this shape. Look out for one in bloom – the very earliest flowering plants to appear on earth had flowers like this.

SHIPS AND TREES

Without trees there would have been no sailing ships. But without sailing ships, there would be far fewer species of tree growing in our parks and gardens today. Many of our large trees were grown from a seed brought back on a sailing ship centuries ago.

A BRANCH OF HISTORY

The oldest immigrant here is sweet bay, brought from the Mediterranean in the sixteenth century, and often seen as a shrub. Tulip tree seeds arrived from North America in the seventeenth century, and evergreen magnolia followed in the eighteenth century but is much rarer because it is sensitive to cold. In the nineteenth century pittosporum came from New Zealand, and the first katsura tree seeds from Japan. Both are still quite rare.

The sweet bay is also called the true laurel, and it was the leaves of this tree that were used to make laurel wreathes in Ancient Greece and Rome. Being crowned with a laurel wreath was the highest honour, and the modern title 'poet laureate' is a reminder of this.

KATSURA TREE ▽
Cercidiphyllum japonicum
Ll 7–10cm. Other trees have heart-shaped leaves, but not arranged in pairs like this. The flowers are reddish but inconspicuous.

SWEET BAY ▲
Laurus nobilis
Ll 5–10cm. Would not grow to full tree-size in Britain. Look for purplish red young twigs, and dark red veins on the leaf near the leaf stalk.

▽ EVERGREEN MAGNOLIA
Magnolia grandiflora
Ll 8–16cm. Quite often seen growing against a wall, only rarely as a tree in Britain. Large, thick, glossy leaves are distinctive.

PITTOSPORUM ▲
Pittosporum tenuifolium
Ll 1–7cm. Some other trees have leaves with crinkly edges (e.g. beech) but none are as crinkly as this. In May, the sweetly scented flowers are unmistakable.

PEARS AND MEDLAR

ROSE FAMILY TREES

The huge family of plants called the Rosaceae includes not just roses, but also many trees. Some of these are shown on the next 18 pages. These rose-family trees tend to have sweet juicy fruits that tempt birds to eat them and so disperse the seeds. Many of these trees have been cultivated for thousands of years, and the fruits made larger and sweeter by plant breeders. It is trees of the rose family that give us pears, apples, apricots, plums and cherries.

FOOD FOR BIRDS

The fruits of other rose-family trees, such as hawthorns, rowans and whitebeams, are a good source of food for wild birds. Cultivated fruit such as pears and apples will also be eaten by larger species, such as blackbirds and thrushes.

The medlar has been grown in Britain for its fruit for over 400 years. The fruits are delicious but they have to be over-ripe and slightly rotten before they are edible. Today medlars are grown solely for their beautiful snow-white flowers, which are unusually large for single tree flowers.

COMMON PEAR
Pyrus communis
Ll 5–8cm. Pears and apples can easily be told apart: the pear is quite a tall tree, whereas the apple is short, with a compact rounded crown. Pear bark cracks into small squares.

WILLOW-LEAVED PEAR
Pyrus salicifolia
Ll 3–9cm. Seen in parks and botanic gardens. No willow has blossom like this. If no flowers or fruit, note that the leaves are smaller, thicker and hairier (when young) than any willow.

PLYMOUTH PEAR ▷
Pyrus cordata
Ll 5–8cm. A wild tree, not considered a true species by some experts. The fruits are tiny, less than 2cm long.

SNOWY MESPIL ▽
Amelanchier ovalis
Ll 2–5cm. Rarely grows to tree size. Quite common in gardens, and occasionally seen growing wild.

MEDLAR △
Mespilus germanica
Ll 5–18cm. A lovely tree from the Mediterranean, low-growing with widely spreading branches. It is grown in parks and gardens but is not common.

APPLES

NATIVE FRUITS

Most of the fruit we eat comes from trees or bushes that originated far away, in foreign lands. The apple is unusual because its wild ancestor is a native tree, known as the crab apple. It can still be found growing in hedge-rows and woods today. If you find one, try to imagine that you are an early farmer, thousands of years ago, looking at this tree and wondering if you should try to grow one near your hut. Then compare a modern apple with the little 'crabs' on the tree – their direct ancestors.

DECORATIVE APPLES

Many kinds of apple tree are grown, not for food, but for the pretty appearance of their flowers or fruit. They are common as street trees in the suburbs. Most are known as 'crab apples' because they have small fruit like the wild tree.

Apple trees are pollinated by bees and other insects. But these trees are not generally self-fertile – which means that the pollen must come from a tree of a different variety, or the flowers will not set fruit. To get over this problem, at least two different varieties of apple should be planted together.

PURPLE CRAB APPLE
Malus X purpurea
Ll 3–10cm. The 'X' shows that this is a hybrid tree, bred by crossing two species. Its fruit and flowers are a purple colour.

CULTIVATED APPLE
Malus domestica
Ll 4–13cm. Many different varieties, but the blossom is always white or pink, with incurved petals. Pear blossom is pure white and the trees are much taller.

GOLDEN HORNET
Malus 'Golden Hornet'
Ll 3–10cm. The bright yellow fruits are distinctive. Used as an ornamental tree.

JOHN DOWNIE CRAB APPLE
Malus 'John Downie'
Ll 3–10cm. Another ornamental variety of the wild crab apple. The fruits are about 3cm long and a striking red or orange, with glossy skin.

ROWANS

ROWAN
Sorbus aucuparia
Ll 3–6cm. Also known as mountain ash. A pretty tree, whether sprouting from a rocky mountainside or growing on a city street. Easily identified in the wild.

GENERAL FEATURES

The rowans are a distinctive group of trees, all with a 'pinnate leaf', that is, one made up of many small leaflets. Leaves like this are also seen on ash, walnut, false acacia and tree of heaven, but rowan leaves are smaller and neater, as are the trees themselves. At most times of year rowans also have blossom or berries to help identification.

CLOSE COUSINS

Rowans are close cousins of the whitebeams (p.90) as you can see by looking at the flowers and fruit. Only the leaves are really different, and even this difference is only 'skin deep' as the hybrids between rowans and whitebeams reveal. They show that a pinnate leaf is really just an ordinary lobed leaf in which the lobes are divided right to the central vein.

The other name for rowan, mountain ash, refers to its capacity for survival high up on mountainsides. Sometimes the trees sprout from narrow fissures in a rocky hillside, where the seed has been dropped by a bird.

SARGENT'S ROWAN
Sorbus sargentiana
Ll 2–5cm. Extra-large leaves for a rowan, up to 35cm long, and with only 9–11 outsized leaflets.

◄UPEH ROWAN ▷
Sorbus hupehensis
Ll 3–8cm. A tree that everyone notices because the berries are white or pale pink. When not in fruit, look or the silvery leaves.

PROJECT

Find a rowan tree (or a whitebeam) and watch to see which birds come down to eat the berries. Keep a record every day, from the time when the berries first turn red until most or all of them have disappeared. How important do you think these berries are to birds? Which birds visit most often? Compare the native rowan with various exotic species planted in parks – do they all attract as many birds?

'JOSEPH ROCK' ▲
***Sorbus* 'Joseph Rock'**
Ll 2–3cm. From China. It has yellow berries and up to 19 tiny leaflets on each leaf, turning brilliant orange or purple in autumn.

WHITEBEAMS & SERVICE TREES

GENERAL FEATURES

The clusters of small, white, five-petalled flowers are typical of whitebeams, service trees and rowans – and rowans are easily distinguished by their pinnate leaves (see p.88). The only similar flowers are seen on hawthorns and cockspur thorns, but these are slightly larger, with fewer in each cluster.

HABITATS

Whitebeam is a native tree, but it only grows in a few areas on limestone or chalk hillside, in Europe. Wild service tree is also native. Whitebeam is easy to find, however, as it is widely planted in parks and gardens, and along suburban streets. The bastard service tree is also seen on city streets, but is an artificial hybrid between rowan and whitebeam.

Beer tree
The name of the true service tree comes from a Roman word for an alcoholic drink that was brewed from its fruits, *cerevisia*. The fruits were mixed with wheat or barley before fermentation, so the drink was something like beer, something like cider. The Spanish word for beer, *cerveca* (pronounced 'servaysa'), comes from the same root.

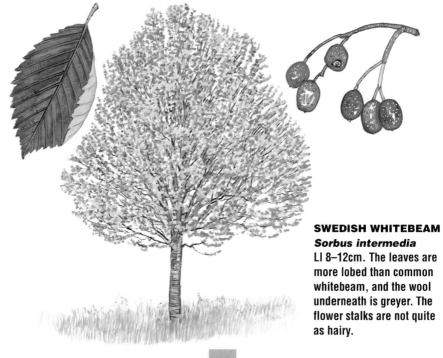

SWEDISH WHITEBEAM
Sorbus intermedia
Ll 8–12cm. The leaves are more lobed than common whitebeam, and the wool underneath is greyer. The flower stalks are not quite as hairy.

BASTARD SERVICE ▼ TREE
Sorbus X thuringiaca
Ll 3–4cm (leaflet).
Unmistakable leaves – half rowan, half whitebeam. Look out for a variety with up-swept branches ('fastigiate' – like a Lombardy poplar), often planted on streets.

TRUE SERVICE TREE ▲
Sorbus domestica
Ll 3–6cm. A rare introduction from southern Europe. Leaves like rowan, but buds are green, glossy and resin-ous – rowan are dull purple.

WHITEBEAM ▼
Sorbus aria
Ll 5–12cm. The only other tree with white wool underneath is white poplar and its leaf shape is quite different.

WILD SERVICE TREE ▲
Sorbus torminalis
Ll 5–10cm. This tree can grow up to 20m high. A native of much of Europe.

HAWTHORNS & COCKSPURS

HAWTHORN
Crataegus monogyna
Ll 2–5cm. The small 3- or 5-lobed leaves are unique among native trees: only field maple leaves (p.107) are vaguely similar in shape, but they are larger and softer. Native throughout Europe.

TREE OF LEGENDS

The hawthorn is one of our most successful trees, found in hedges and fields all over the countryside. Its blossom was once used in the May-Day celebrations, on May 1st, and hawthorn is also known as 'may'. A variety of hawthorn, called the Glastonbury Thorn, flowers very early, sometimes in mid-winter. Legend has it that it flowers on Christmas Day itself.

NATIVE AND INTRODUCED

Hawthorn is a native tree (and more often a shrub) but there are also cultivated varieties grown in parks and on roadsides. Cockspur thorns are all introduced from North America, and they too are widely planted along suburban streets or in landscaped gardens.

Useful trees
Hawthorns can be laid to make hedges, by bending the young shoots sideways and weaving them together. The many thorns deter cows from breaking through. Hawthorn fruits, called haws, help birds through the winter, and the leaves and haws nourish many insects. In Britain, 150 different species feed on them, and on the continent, the number is even higher, 230 species.

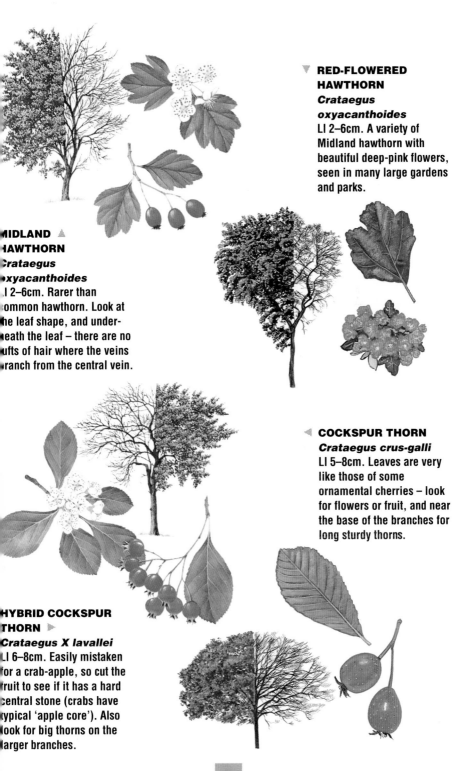

RED-FLOWERED HAWTHORN
Crataegus oxyacanthoides
Ll 2–6cm. A variety of Midland hawthorn with beautiful deep-pink flowers, seen in many large gardens and parks.

MIDLAND HAWTHORN
Crataegus oxyacanthoides
Ll 2–6cm. Rarer than common hawthorn. Look at the leaf shape, and underneath the leaf – there are no tufts of hair where the veins branch from the central vein.

COCKSPUR THORN
Crataegus crus-galli
Ll 5–8cm. Leaves are very like those of some ornamental cherries – look for flowers or fruit, and near the base of the branches for long sturdy thorns.

HYBRID COCKSPUR THORN ▶
Crataegus X lavallei
Ll 6–8cm. Easily mistaken for a crab-apple, so cut the fruit to see if it has a hard central stone (crabs have typical 'apple core'). Also look for big thorns on the larger branches.

ORNAMENTAL CHERRIES

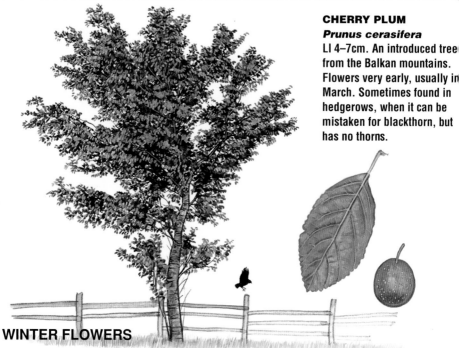

CHERRY PLUM
Prunus cerasifera
Ll 4–7cm. An introduced tree from the Balkan mountains. Flowers very early, usually in March. Sometimes found in hedgerows, when it can be mistaken for blackthorn, but has no thorns.

WINTER FLOWERS

You will not find any of these trees growing in the wild, but they are all used to brighten up city streets or gardens. All the trees shown here flower very early, and the autumn-flowering cherry may produce blossom all through the winter. Gardeners and town-planners value them highly for providing cheerful colour in the darkest months of the year.

OUT TOO EARLY

Flowers bloom when they do for good reason. If they need to be pollinated by insects, they open when those insects are about. The very earliest wild trees to flower, such as hazel, can come out before the insects because they are wind pollinated. Ornamental cherries, that have been persuaded by plant-breeders to flower in winter, rarely set fruit, and often the blossom is spoiled by frost.

Leaves can only do their job if they contain the green pigment chlorophyll. Purple leaves, like those of purple-leaved plum or copper beech, contain chlorophyll, but they also have other, darker pigments, which mask the green colour. Such trees are ornamentals, produced by plant breeders.

PURPLE-LEAVED PLUM ▽
Prunus cerasifera
'Atropurpurea'
Ll 3–6cm. Bright coppery leaves and white flowers in early spring, with leaves turning dull purplish red later in the year.

PURPLE-LEAVED ▲ PLUM
Prunus cerasifera
'Nigra'
Ll 3–6cm. A pink-flowered variety of the purple-leaved plum.

AUTUMN-FLOWERING ▲ CHERRY
Prunus subhirtella
'Autumnalis'
Ll 3–6cm. Small, delicate leaves and flowers. This cherry is unique because it sometimes begins flowering even before winter sets in.

PROJECT

Find two or more autumn-flowering cherries or purple-leaved plums growing nearby. Each year, record when they start to flower, and how long flowering goes on for. Keep a record of the weather from autumn through to spring as well. Do this for at least three years. Does the weather affect flowering? Do young trees differ from older ones? If you also keep a record of some pussy willows, blackthorns and hazels (they too flower very early) you can compare the effects of the weather on them.

ORNAMENTAL CHERRIES

SOUR CHERRY
Prunus cerasus
LI 3–8cm. The fruit of this tree is the Morello cherry, used in drinks and jam. The fact that it bears fruit at all distinguishes it from the sterile Japanese cherries.

SINGLES AND DOUBLES

Wild cherries and their relatives all have single flowers – with just one circle of petals, numbering five altogether. Many ornamental blossom trees have double flowers, with two or more circles of petals, one inside the other. There may be dozens of petals in such flowers.

FLOWERS BUT NO FRUIT

Because Japanese cherries are largely sterile, they cannot be grown from seed. Instead they are cultivated by taking cuttings or by a process known as budding. This is done by cutting out a bud and inserting it into the stem of a wild cherry. If the bud grows (and the process does not always work) the branches of the wild cherry are later removed, and the grafted cherry takes over.

Japanese cherries are the products of very intense breeding programmes. One result is that the flowers are for show only – they can no longer set fruit. Some of these sterile flowers have even lost the normal female organs – instead there are tiny green leaves at the centre of each bloom.

JAPANESE CHERRIES
Prunus serrulata
LI 8–20cm. Only one species, but with so many different varieties that to say 'Japanese cherry' would be misleading. Identifying all the different varieties is very difficult – just enjoy the blossom instead.

DOUBLE CHERRY PLUM
Prunus X blireana
LI 6–8cm. A hybrid, one of whose parents was the purple-leaved plum. It has the same dark leaves, but the pink flowers are double.

YOSHINO CHERRY
Prunus X yedoensis
LI 8–20cm. Also from Japan, but a different hybrid from the Japanese cherries. The twigs are downy at first, unlike Japanese cherry twigs.

'Amanogawa'
LI 8–20cm. A variety of Japanese cherry with upswept branches like a Lombardy poplar, rising to a pointed top ('fastigiate').

'Longipes'
LI 8–20cm. Although the pink-flowered Japanese cherries are more widely planted there are also many white-flowered varieties.

WEEPING JAPANESE CHERRY
Kikushidare Sakura'
LI 8–12cm. A small tree with blossom-laden branches hanging almost to the ground.

PLUMS, CHERRIES & SLOES

GENERAL FEATURES

Unless there are fruits on the tree, it can be very difficult to recognize some cherries and their relatives. Plums have dullish leaves and dark, dull, rough bark, unlike the larger cherries. Apples and pears have slightly woolly leaves and stems, with five styles in each flower, not just one. Cherry leaves (wild, Sargent's and Japanese cherries) often have two small red 'glands' on the stalk near the base of the leaf. The buds grow in dense clusters.

The pale blue dusty 'bloom' on the surface of sloes (blackthorn fruits) is a layer of yeast cells. These yeasts live on the surface of all fruits, feeding on their sugars, but the bloom can only be seen on dark-skinned fruits like sloes and plums.

GLOSSY BARK

With the Japanese cherries, Sargent's cherry and wild cherry, the bark is a useful identification feature. It may be restricted to just a small part of the trunk or large branches, but somewhere you will find glossy red-brown bark broken up by straight horizontal lines of warty bumps.

BLACKTHORN
Prunus spinosa

Ll 2–5cm. Also known as sloe. A native shrub and very common. Tough little leaves and long thorns with buds on them make it quite easy to recognize. The 'dusty' blue sloes (fruits) are unmistakable.

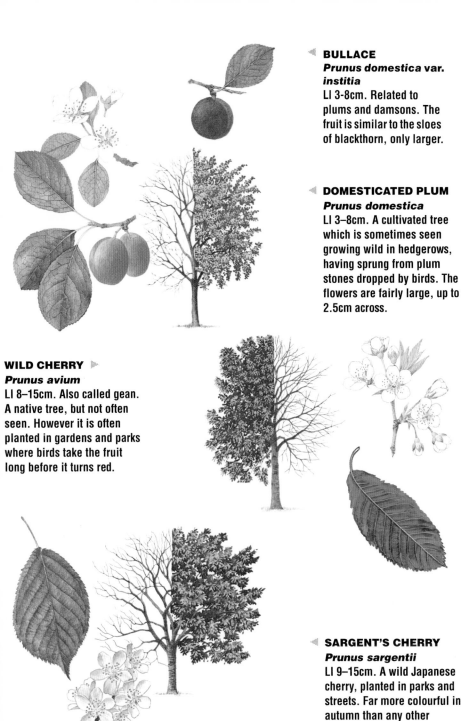

BULLACE
Prunus domestica var. _institia_
LI 3-8cm. Related to plums and damsons. The fruit is similar to the sloes of blackthorn, only larger.

DOMESTICATED PLUM
Prunus domestica
LI 3–8cm. A cultivated tree which is sometimes seen growing wild in hedgerows, having sprung from plum stones dropped by birds. The flowers are fairly large, up to 2.5cm across.

WILD CHERRY ▷
Prunus avium
LI 8–15cm. Also called gean. A native tree, but not often seen. However it is often planted in gardens and parks where birds take the fruit long before it turns red.

SARGENT'S CHERRY
Prunus sargentii
LI 9–15cm. A wild Japanese cherry, planted in parks and streets. Far more colourful in autumn than any other cherry; may turn bright red as early as September.

ALMONDS AND SPIKE CHERRIES

ALMOND
Prunus dulcis
Ll 4–13cm. Easily identified when the dull green 'fruits' appear. In spring, note that the flowers are larger than any other of this group. The blackish bark and untidy branches are characteristic.

GENERAL FEATURES

A few species of cherry have their flowers grouped together on a stalk – these are known to botanists as flower 'spikes' even though they may hang downwards. One of the 'spike-flowered cherries', the bird cherry, is a native tree but most are exotic species that are sensitive to cold and do not grow into proper trees in Britain. Two are evergreens, the Portugal laurel and the cherry laurel.

NAMES AND RELATIONSHIPS

The scientific names of plants and animals are useful sources of information. The first word of the name is called the generic name. If two trees have the same generic name, it shows that they are closely related. The fact that almond is *Prunus dulcis* shows that it is closely related to the cherries (which are all *Prunus*), even though it is not called a cherry.

When bird cherries are grown in parks and gardens, it is not the true wild form that is planted but one of the cultivated varieties. These have been artificially bred to have larger flowers than the wild bird cherry.

BIRD CHERRY
Prunus padus
LI 6–10cm. A pretty native tree (though rarely seen in the wild) with delicate leaves and long skeins of white flowers. Has smooth dull bark.

BLACK CHERRY ▶
Prunus serotina
LI 5–14cm. Also called rum cherry. An American tree, planted widely in Europe. The bark is purplish grey on top, peeling off to a pinkish brown underlayer. On old trees the bark is scented.

CHERRY LAUREL ▼
Prunus laurocerasus
LI 10–20cm. Widely grown as a hedge, but rarely reaching tree size in Britain. Crushed leaves once used by insect collectors to kill their specimens.

PORTUGAL LAUREL ▲
Prunus lusitanica
LI 8–13cm. Often used for hedging, and sometimes making a tree in frost-free regions. Larger flowers on longer spikes than cherry laurel.

EXOTIC FRUIT TREES

TREE FAMILIES

Shown here are the last two trees of the cherry family, peach and apricot. These are also the last two of the rose family, a huge group that includes apples, hawthorns, rowans and cherries. By contrast, the strawberry tree belongs to a family with few other trees in it, the heather family. Look at its flowers to see the resemblance to heather. There are many other trees in the family to which the orange belongs, but you will only find them in Mediterranean areas as they all need a warm climate.

BRILLIANT BARK

There are other species of strawberry tree that are sometimes grown in botanic gardens and large parks. Some lose their bark to reveal bare areas underneath, which may be shiny and brightly coloured. One is a rich gleaming red.

Surviving frost
When water freezes, it forms crystals that have sharp points. These puncture cell membranes, which kills the cell. Plants that are resistant to frost have special chemicals inside the cell which either stop water from freezing or control the shape of the crystals. Many of our ornamental trees come from warmer climates, and some have no defence against frost. The strawberry tree is unusual because it is a frost-sensitive native tree, growing wild on the frost-free west coast of Ireland.

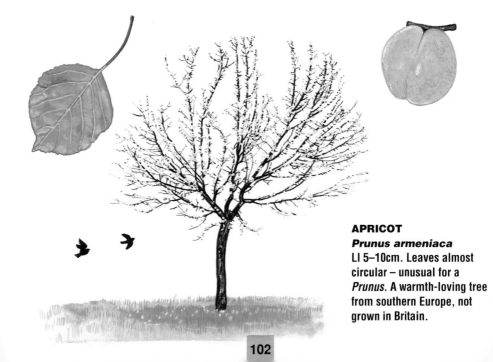

APRICOT
Prunus armeniaca
Ll 5–10cm. Leaves almost circular – unusual for a *Prunus*. A warmth-loving tree from southern Europe, not grown in Britain.

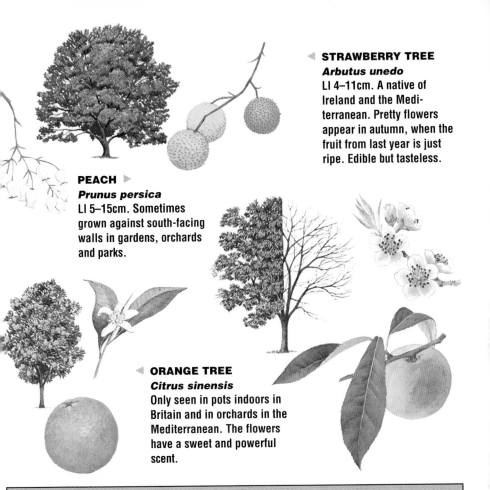

STRAWBERRY TREE
Arbutus unedo
LI 4–11cm. A native of Ireland and the Mediterranean. Pretty flowers appear in autumn, when the fruit from last year is just ripe. Edible but tasteless.

PEACH
Prunus persica
LI 5–15cm. Sometimes grown against south-facing walls in gardens, orchards and parks.

ORANGE TREE
Citrus sinensis
Only seen in pots indoors in Britain and in orchards in the Mediterranean. The flowers have a sweet and powerful scent.

PROJECT

The fruit trees shown here can all be grown from seeds. You will need a sunny windowsill, or a conservatory, to start with. For peach and apricot, choose ripe fruit and soak the stones for 48 hours. If the shell is still hard, crack it, but be very gentle or you will damage the seed inside. Plant in a peat pot, so that you can later plant it out easily – they dislike having their roots disturbed. Peach trees can eventually be planted outside, but only against a sunny, south-facing wall. Of the oranges, mandarins and tangerines are the best for growing in pots.

PEA FAMILY TREES

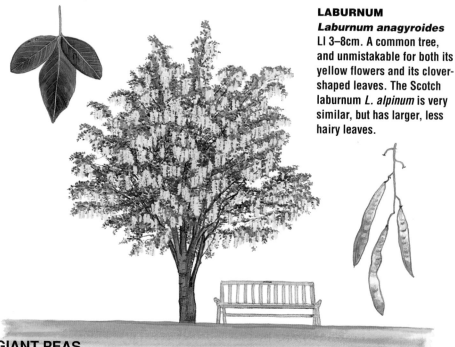

LABURNUM
Laburnum anagyroides
Ll 3–8cm. A common tree, and unmistakable for both its yellow flowers and its clover-shaped leaves. The Scotch laburnum *L. alpinum* is very similar, but has larger, less hairy leaves.

GIANT PEAS

Apart from the tree of heaven, all the trees on this page belong to the pea family. You will see how similar all the flowers and pods are. Laburnum even smells the same – scratch the twigs and they smell like runner beans, but beware, it is very poisonous.

LEGENDARY NAMES

The Judas tree comes from the Mediterranean, where, according to legend, it is the tree on which Judas Iscariot hanged himself. The false acacia is also called the locust tree, because the early settlers of North America found its beans useful for feeding their animals, and named it after the locust (or carob tree) of the Bible. Tree of heaven was called 'tree that grows to the sky' by the Chinese because it is so tall. This was translated into 'tree of heaven'.

Wattle is a name used for acacias in Australia. An old English word, it describes a flat, lightweight material produced by weaving hazel stems between larger branches. It could be used for making fences, and when the first settlers in Australia needed fences, they used this ancient method, but used acacia stems instead.

SILVER WATTLE ▽
Acacia dealbata
Ll 3–6mm. Widely grown around the Mediterranean. Rare in Britain, except in frost-free areas. Acacias are sometimes seen in botanic gardens and large parks.

TREE OF HEAVEN ▲
Ailanthus altissima
Ll 7–12cm. Notice the two 'teeth' on each leaflet – these, and the red leaf-stalk, mark it out from ash.

◁ FALSE ACACIA
Robinia pseudacacia
Ll 2–5cm. A tree seen in parks or around old houses – few young trees seen. If unsure, look for the massive sinuous ridges on the bark, and the thorns on some twigs, especially sprouts from the trunk.

JUDAS TREE ▷
Cercis siliquastrum
Ll 7–12cm. A small, leaning tree, with smooth-edged, silky, almost circular leaves. Some flowers sprout straight from the trunk and branches.

MAPLES AND PLANES

LONDON PLANE
Platanus X hispanica
LI 2–20cm. A beautiful tree,
named for its widespread
use in central London (and
other cities) where it is one
of the few trees to withstand
the air pollution.

GENERAL FEATURES

Shown here are two groups of trees which are
not related but have similar leaves. The trick to
identifying such trees is to know what other
features to look for. In this case it is the
arrangement of the buds on the twigs. In maples
there are always two together, in pairs. The
leaves sprout from the buds, so they are paired
up as well. Such buds are 'opposite', while the
planes show 'alternate'.

TREES AND CITIES

Plane trees have thin bark that peels off in small
scales. This may be one factor in their resistance
to the air pollution of cities (by allowing the
bark to shed soot) but it cannot be the whole
story. Sycamores in the countryside often have
black spots on the leaves, caused by a fungus.
These are never seen on city sycamores, because
the fungus cannot survive in polluted air.

Young plane leaves are
covered in a layer of fine,
spiky golden hairs which
help to keep insects from
feeding on them. In time,
most leaves develop
chemicals with an
unpleasant taste that keep
insects at bay, but young
leaves lack these.

SYCAMORE ▽
Acer pseudoplatanus
Ll 10–15cm. The commonest maple in Britain, seeding furiously and springing up everywhere. Large, dull, leathery leaves with deep-set veins. The buds are very large, their scales green with a brown border.

◢ ORIENTAL PLANE
Platanus orientalis
Ll 10–18cm. Much less common than London plane – notice that the leaves are more deeply cut. One of the parents of the hybrid London plane – the other was American plane.

◁ FIELD MAPLE
Acer campestre
Ll 4–12cm. Much smaller leaves than other maples, thin and silky in spring, often red or orange in autumn. Common in hedgerows in northern Europe.

NORWAY MAPLE ▷
Acer platanoides
Ll 10–15cm. Not a native tree, but widely naturalised. The only similar, widespread maple is sycamore, but Norway maple's leaves are much thinner, smoother and more delicate.

INTRODUCED MAPLES

GENERAL FEATURES

All maples have winged seeds, and their buds and leaves in opposite pairs. Three of the trees shown here belong to a distinctive group called the snake-bark maples. In fact 'zebra-bark' would be a better name, as the narrow stripes on the bark are zebra-like, except in colour – they are usually white on green. Most of these maples come from China or Japan.

Maple syrup
Maple syrup is made from a species of maple called the sugar maple that is native to North America, and rarely grown in Great Britain. The syrup is made from the tree's sugar-rich sap, which is intercepted as it flows down the trunk.

AUTUMN COLOURS

In the United States and Canada the maples are noted for their 'fall colors' (autumn colours), which people travel miles to see. Among the trees that produce these eye-catching displays are the red maples, but when grown in Europe they rarely manage more than a dull orange. The reasons for this are not entirely understood, but the long hot summer of eastern North America probably makes a difference.

PÈRE DAVID'S MAPLE
Acer davidii
Ll 5–15cm. A small tree, the most widely planted of the snake-bark maples. Difficult to identify exactly as it has several forms with quite differently shaped leaves.

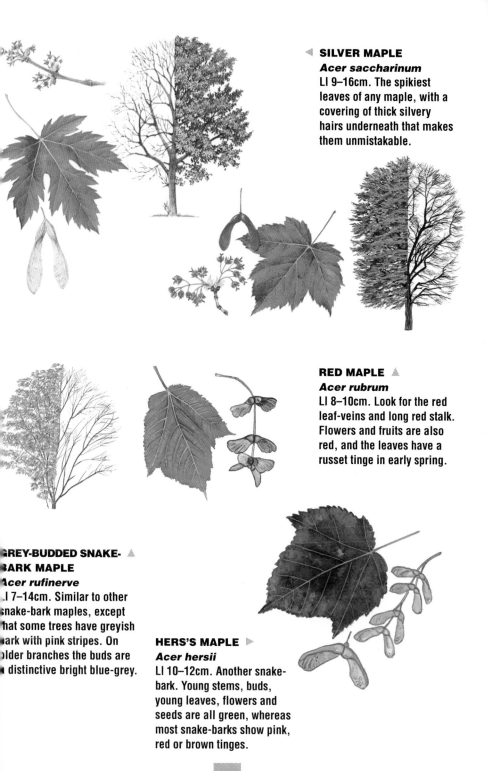

SILVER MAPLE
Acer saccharinum
Ll 9–16cm. The spikiest leaves of any maple, with a covering of thick silvery hairs underneath that makes them unmistakable.

RED MAPLE
Acer rubrum
Ll 8–10cm. Look for the red leaf-veins and long red stalk. Flowers and fruits are also red, and the leaves have a russet tinge in early spring.

GREY-BUDDED SNAKE-BARK MAPLE
Acer rufinerve
Ll 7–14cm. Similar to other snake-bark maples, except that some trees have greyish bark with pink stripes. On older branches the buds are a distinctive bright blue-grey.

HERS'S MAPLE
Acer hersii
Ll 10–12cm. Another snake-bark. Young stems, buds, young leaves, flowers and seeds are all green, whereas most snake-barks show pink, red or brown tinges.

109

MAPLES AND SWEET GUM

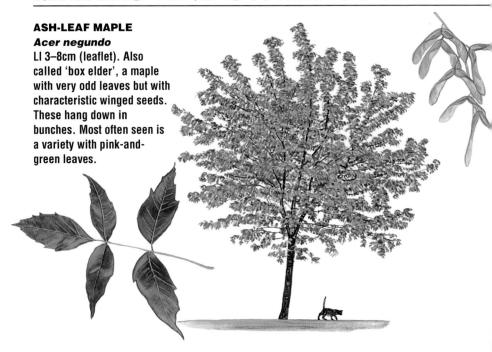

ASH-LEAF MAPLE
Acer negundo
Ll 3–8cm (leaflet). Also called 'box elder', a maple with very odd leaves but with characteristic winged seeds. These hang down in bunches. Most often seen is a variety with pink-and-green leaves.

JAPANESE MAPLES

Many ornamental trees have been bred in Japan, but the Japanese maples are the most exceptional of these, with their small size, lacy foliage, and gnarled, leaning trunks. They are the only maples to develop their full autumn colours in our cool damp climate. Try collecting seeds and germinating them – you can grow these lovely little trees in a large pot.

VARIEGATED LEAVES

The variety of ash-leaved maple that is most often seen has 'variegated' leaves. This means that they have some white areas (or in this case, pink). Because the green pigment in leaves is the part that makes food, variegated leaves are less efficient. Wild trees do not have such leaves (though some wild plants do) because they could not sustain the tree's growth.

Autumn colours develop because deciduous trees withdraw the green pigment chlorophyll from their leaves and store the vital nutrients it contains. This exposes other pigments, called carotenoids, which are yellow. In some trees, the yellow carotenoids then change to orange or red.

DOWNY JAPANESE MAPLE ▽

Acer japonicum

Ll 7–13cm. The name comes from the hairy leaf-stalks. Less deeply lobed leaves than smooth Japanese maple, with 7–11 lobes per leaf. Leaf colour varies.

SMOOTH JAPANESE MAPLE ▲

Acer palmatum

Ll 7–9cm. Look for the hairless leaf-stalks, but also count the leaf lobes: there are 5–7, and they are more deeply cut than in downy Japanese maple. The colour varies greatly.

PAPER-BARK MAPLE ▷

Acer griseum

Ll 6–10cm. An introduction from China, grown for its bark, which peels off in thin papery strips to expose a glossy chestnut-brown surface below. Notice the unusual leaf-shape.

SWEET GUM ▷

Liquidambar styraciflua

Ll 7–15cm. Not a maple, but sometimes mistaken for one. Notice that the buds and leaves are alternate, not opposite. Crush a young leaf or bud and sniff – there is a pleasant balsamy smell.

TREES WITH LARGE FLOWERS

HORSE CHESTNUT
Aesculus
hippocastanum
Ll 10–25cm. Instantly recognizable. The only similar tree that you may see is Indian horse-chestnut. Large leaves which are divided like a hand.

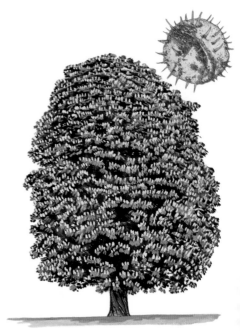

FLOWERS AND INSECTS

Plants have large showy flowers to attract insects such as bees, butterflies or hoverflies. The flowers contain sugary nectar on which the insects feed, but they also contain pollen, which brushes onto the insect's body as it feeds. When the insect visits another flower, some of the pollen brushes off, and this may 'fertilize' that flower, so that it can set seed.

WIND OR INSECTS

Pollen can also be spread by the wind, and this is a method that many trees use – because they are tall, the wind blows their branches around, and this disperses the pollen. Trees which need insects to spread their pollen are usually smaller trees, or those which sometimes grow in isolated spots, such as mountain ash (rowan), or which grow in the lower storeys of forests, where the wind does not stir them.

The buds of horse-chestnut have a thick sticky coating, which has earned them the name 'sticky-buds'. The coating protects the leaves inside the bud from hungry insects, by snaring their legs or wings. Occasionally, small birds have become stuck to the buds.

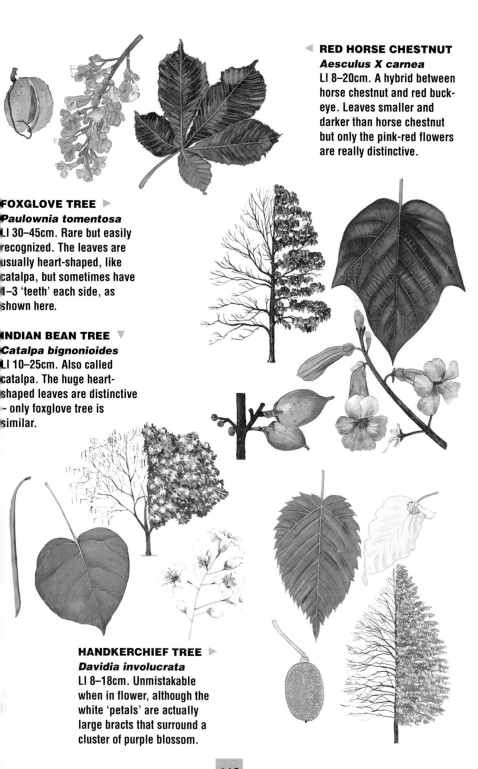

RED HORSE CHESTNUT
Aesculus X carnea
Ll 8–20cm. A hybrid between horse chestnut and red buckeye. Leaves smaller and darker than horse chestnut but only the pink-red flowers are really distinctive.

FOXGLOVE TREE ▷
Paulownia tomentosa
Ll 30–45cm. Rare but easily recognized. The leaves are usually heart-shaped, like catalpa, but sometimes have 1–3 'teeth' each side, as shown here.

INDIAN BEAN TREE ▽
Catalpa bignonioides
Ll 10–25cm. Also called catalpa. The huge heart-shaped leaves are distinctive – only foxglove tree is similar.

HANDKERCHIEF TREE ▷
Davidia involucrata
Ll 8–18cm. Unmistakable when in flower, although the white 'petals' are actually large bracts that surround a cluster of purple blossom.

HOLLY, BOX AND EUCALYPTUS

EVERGREEN OR DECIDUOUS

Some trees drop all their leaves once a year, and go into a dormant state – either to survive a cold winter, or a very dry season. Other trees keep each leaf for three or four years, so saving energy. And the leaves do not all fall at once, so the tree is always making food.

ARMOURED LEAVES

The problem for evergreen trees is that their leaves must not get damaged, unlike the 'disposable' leaves of deciduous trees which are thrown away every year. So the leaves are very tough and leathery to keep insects out, and they may have prickles to stop deer eating them, as holly has. Others have invisible chemical defences to stop insects eating them – these are what give gum trees their distinctive scent.

Holly leaves are inedible to most insects, but the flowers and berries are eaten by the caterpillar of the holly blue butterfly. Look out for berries with tiny holes – they will have been hollowed out by very young caterpillars feeding inside them. Adult butterflies are a deep violet blue colour.

HOLLY
Ilex aquifolium
LI 5–12cm. If found in woodland, there is no mistaking our native holly, but in gardens it may be confused with introduced hollies, or even with other shrubs with similar leaves.

BOX ▲
Buxus sempervirens
LI 1–3cm. Rarely seen in the wild, except in specific areas, but often in garden hedges. Notice the way the leaf-edges curl under – a characteristic feature.

RHODODENDRON ▲
Rhododendron ponticum
LI 10–20cm. An Asian shrub, once much planted in woods to provide cover for game-birds such as pheasants. Even when not in flower, the rosettes of glossy leaves are unmistakable.

CIDER GUM ▲
Eucalyptus gunnii
LI 4–7cm. The most widely planted eucalyptus in Britain. It comes from the highlands of Tasmania, so is hardier than other eucalyptus, surviving frosts.

TASMANIAN BLUE ▶ GUM
Eucalyptus globulus
LI 10–30cm. Also called southern blue gum. Vulnerable to frost.

SPINDLE TREES & BUCKTHORNS

SPINDLE TREE
Euonymus europaeus
Ll 5–10cm. A native shrub which is common in much of Europe. It is very noticeable in the autumn with its garishly coloured fruits and purple-orange leaves.

NAMES AND USES

Many trees and shrubs were once used, not just for wood, but as a source of medicines, dyes, and other items. Alder buckthorn was among the most useful. The bark made yellow-brown dyes, and charcoal from its wood was vital for making gunpowder. Both the buckthorns contain drugs used as purgatives (laxatives). Spindle tree is so called because its hard white wood was made into spindles for spinning wool.

POISONOUS BERRIES

We know that plants have bright, conspicuous berries to persuade animals to eat them and so disperse the seed. But many berries are poisonous to humans or have dire effects – buckthorn berries are laxatives, while spindle berries would make you violently sick. Why? The answer is that birds make better dispersers than mammals, so plants equip the berries with chemicals that the birds can stomach but mammals (including humans) cannot.

Spindle fruits are unusual in that they split open while still on the tree to reveal the seeds within. As the fruits are pink and the seeds orange, this creates an eye-catching display.

ALDER BUCKTHORN ▷
Frangula alnus
Ll 3–7cm. A native shrub, but not common, except in particular areas, such as the edges of marshland. The berries are purplish black when ripe.

JAPANESE SPINDLE ▲ TREE
Euonymus japonicus
Ll 3–7cm. Sometimes seen in gardens. Where it has been planted in Europe it has often escaped and now grows wild.

BUCKTHORN ▲
Rhamnus catharticus
Ll 3–7cm. A fairly common shrub. Notice the sharp thorns at the tip of each stem, unlike the thornless alder buckthorn.

HOW TO IDENTIFY

Trees with oval leaves cause the most trouble. Don't despair! Start by only trying to identify such trees if in flower or fruit. Once identified, look at both sides of its leaves, and rub them between your fingers to feel the texture. Crush and sniff the leaves. Inspect the twigs and buds too. In this way you can get to know the trees and will soon be able to identify them, even when there are no flowers or fruit.

Buckthorn   **Spindle**

LIMES

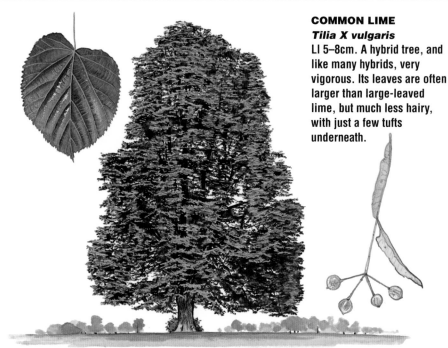

COMMON LIME
Tilia X vulgaris
Ll 5–8cm. A hybrid tree, and like many hybrids, very vigorous. Its leaves are often larger than large-leaved lime, but much less hairy, with just a few tufts underneath.

HEART-SHAPED LEAVES

Limes are not the only trees to have heart-shaped leaves. The Indian bean tree and the foxglove tree both have heart-shaped leaves, but these are very much larger. Hazel sometimes has some leaves that are almost heart-shaped, but these are rough and hairy compared to lime leaves. The most similar leaves are those of mulberry and the handkerchief tree, but both have larger 'teeth' around the edge of the leaf.

SWEET TREES

The flowers of lime trees are collected and used to make a herbal tea with a sweet scent. Lime trees also produce a fine rain of sugary liquid which falls on everything below them. This is because thousands of aphids feed on the trees' sap, extracting nutrients from it and rejecting the rest, which falls as treacly droppings.

Many different caterpillars feed on the leaves of lime, including the lime hawk moth, the September thorn and the orange sallow, all shown here. Lime leaves are so soft and palatable that cattle love to browse on them. Lime tree seedlings are rare in pastureland for this reason.

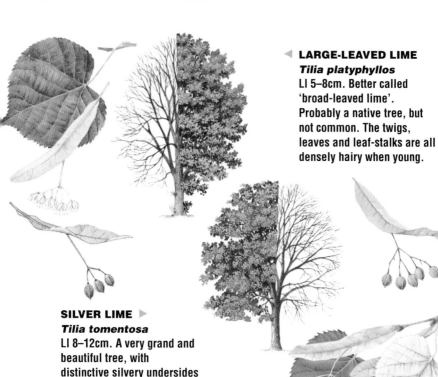

LARGE-LEAVED LIME
Tilia platyphyllos
Ll 5–8cm. Better called 'broad-leaved lime'. Probably a native tree, but not common. The twigs, leaves and leaf-stalks are all densely hairy when young.

SILVER LIME ▷
Tilia tomentosa
Ll 8–12cm. A very grand and beautiful tree, with distinctive silvery undersides to the leaves.

SMALL-LEAVED LIME
Tilia cordata
Ll 2–4cm. Look for a bluish-grey underside to the leaf, with tufts of rust-coloured hair near the central vein.

PROJECT

Lime trees are very strongly scented when they are in flower. Find a flowering lime tree and watch the flowers nearest the ground. Do you see insects visiting them? What sort of insects are they, and how many different kinds are there? Count the number of insects around each flower-cluster and estimate how many there might be around the tree as a whole.

BERRY-BEARING SHRUBS

SPREADING SHRUBS

Apart from cornelian cherry, which is introduced, the other shrubs shown here are common
'pioneers' on waste ground, along woodland
edges, in hedgerows and scrub. Wayfaring tree
was originally called wayfarer's tree, because it
was common by lanes and roads.

ABUNDANT SEEDS

The seeds of these shrubs are spread by birds
eating the berries, but only a tiny percentage of
the berries are lucky enough to fall in a suitable
place and grow into a shrub. That is why each
bush produces hundreds of berries every year. In
its lifetime it will produce thousands, but none
of these may survive. The berries of wayfaring
tree were once used to make a bluish-black ink.
Dogwood berries are waxy, and were once used
to make lamp oil.

You can identify guelder rose
by holding the berries up to
the light. Unlike most
berries, they are translucent,
and shine like beads of red
glass. The only similar
berries are those of red-
currant, which hang down in
long strands, unlike guelder
rose.

GUELDER ROSE
Viburnum opulus
Ll 3–8cm. One of our
prettiest native shrubs. A
variety with flowers like
snowballs grows in gardens.

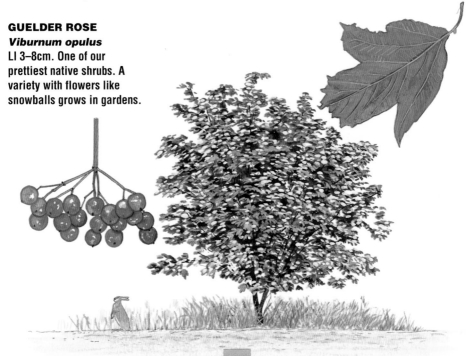

DOGWOOD ▽
Cornus sanguinea
Ll 4–8cm. 'Sanguinea' means 'blood' – look for the blood-red stems. In autumn this red colour extends to the leaves as well.

WAYFARING TREE ▲
Viburnum lantana
Ll 4–14cm. Notable for its clusters of berries, which are often a mixture of colours, some yellow, some red and some dark purple.

CORNELIAN CHERRY ▽
Cornus mas
Ll 4–10cm. A dogwood, but named for its cherry-like fruits. Broken open, they reveal a long, smooth, torpedo-shaped stone.

PROJECT

You can make an interesting record of berry-bearing shrubs by making plaster casts. Press some leaves and berries into modelling clay to make a mould. Use a cardboard tube to contain the plaster of Paris, pouring enough in to make a disc about 2cm thick. When it has set, remove the clay, and paint the leaves and berries with enamel paint. Try to get the colours exact.

ASHES AND ELDERS

ASH

Fraxinus excelsior
Ll 5–12cm. One of the commonest trees of the countryside, also springing up in city gardens. Paired black buds on elegant grey stems are unique.

FERN-LIKE LEAVES

The technical term for leaves like those of ash and elder is 'pinnate'. They are really one large leaf, divided up into many leaflets. Other common trees with pinnate leaves are the rowans, walnuts and wingnuts, tree of heaven, false acacia, wattle (acacia), box elder or ash-leaved maple. The exact shape of the leaflets is used to separate out acacia, false acacia, rowan and tree of heaven. The others can be recognized by their twigs, buds, flowers or fruit.

USEFUL TO WILDLIFE

Elderberries are quickly eaten by birds in the autumn, as they are juicy and sweet. (Humans can eat these berries too, but the slightly soapy taste puts most people off.) Badgers use the light corky bark as a scratching post, to clean soil from their paws after excavating a burrow.

Ash trees on farmland were often pollarded to produce regular crops of long straight stems. Pollarded trees live longer, but often become hollow in old age. This ash has not just become hollow but also split in two – yet it is still alive.

MANNA ASH ▷
Fraxinus ornus
Ll 3–10cm. Leaves like ash but with fewer leaflets (usually 7 rather than 9). The paired buds are onion-shaped, greyish and downy, quite unlike ash. Masses of fluffy white flowers in spring.

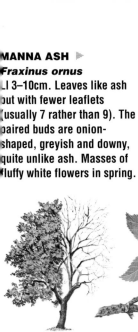

ELDER ▲
Sambucus nigra
Ll 4–12cm (leaflet). The leaves are like ash, but not the buds. Look for the light, corky, deeply ridged bark and corky angular twigs with large breathing pores.

RED-BERRIED ELDER ▽
Sambucus racemosa
Ll 4–12cm. Also called alpine elder, as it is found in mountains. The leaves are more pointed and yellowish than elder. The berries are red when ripe, not black.

◁ LAURUSTINUS
Viburnum tinus
Ll 3–10cm. Note the glossy leaves and unusually shaped, dark blue fruit. A European species, rarely seen in Britain.

FLOWERING SHRUBS

SEA BUCKTHORN
Hippophae rhamnoides
Ll 1–6cm. Only osier has
such slender leaves, and
they are much larger. Few
other shrubs will be found
growing so close to the sea.
Native in most of Europe.

HABITAT

Salt spray and strong winds make life very
difficult for plants beside the sea, especially trees
and shrubs. Two of the shrubs shown here, sea
buckthorn and tamarisk, are particularly
valuable because they can withstand these
difficult conditions. Small tough leaves are useful
for not losing too much moisture, and the leaves
of tamarisk are so small that they do not stick
out from the stem.

GOING WILD

Many trees and shrubs that are not native to
Britain have managed to 'go wild', having first
been planted in gardens or parkland, or on large
estates. Most are not fully suited to the climate,
so they do not spread very much. But some do
almost too well, such as the rhododendrons
which have invaded many woods and crowded
out native plants.

Stomata
Tiny scale-like leaves,
pressed close to the stem,
are an excellent way of
saving moisture. Leaves
have small pores through
which they breathe, called
stomata. These leak water
vapour in all plants, but little
is lost by scale leaves
because the stomata are
held tightly against the stem.
This arrangement is common
in conifers, such as cypress,
but not among broadleaves
making tamarisk highly
unusual.

124

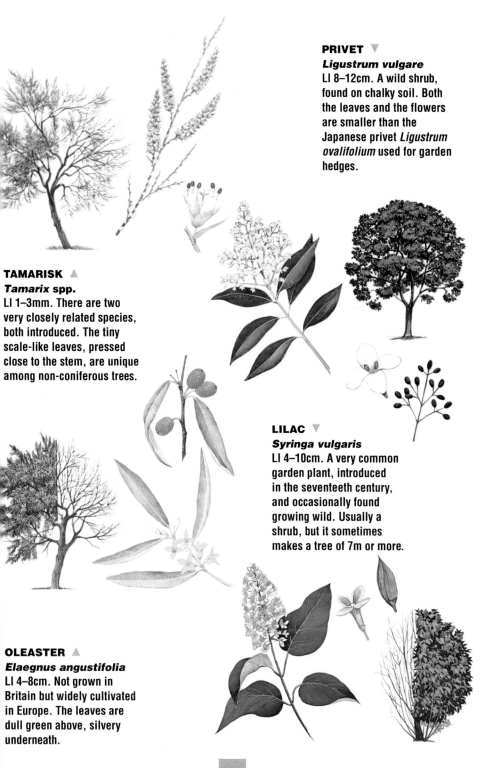

PRIVET ▽
Ligustrum vulgare
Ll 8–12cm. A wild shrub, found on chalky soil. Both the leaves and the flowers are smaller than the Japanese privet *Ligustrum ovalifolium* used for garden hedges.

TAMARISK △
Tamarix spp.
Ll 1–3mm. There are two very closely related species, both introduced. The tiny scale-like leaves, pressed close to the stem, are unique among non-coniferous trees.

LILAC ▽
Syringa vulgaris
Ll 4–10cm. A very common garden plant, introduced in the seventeeth century, and occasionally found growing wild. Usually a shrub, but it sometimes makes a tree of 7m or more.

OLEASTER △
Elaegnus angustifolia
Ll 4–8cm. Not grown in Britain but widely cultivated in Europe. The leaves are dull green above, silvery underneath.

INDEX

ILLUSTRATIONS BY

Fred Anderson 26–27 · Derek Brown 24–25 · Shirley Felts Cover · Maltings Partnership 22–23 · David More 4, 6–7, 8, 11 (top), 17, 28–43, 44, 46, 48, 49 (below left), 52, 54, 55 (below), 56, 57 (below right), 58, 60, 62, 64, 65 (top right), 66, 67 (below right), 68, 69, 70, 71 (below right), 72, 73 (top right), 74, 75 (top left and below right), 76, 77 (below right), 78, 80, 81 (below two right), 82, 84, 86, 87, 88, 89, 90, 92, 93 (top and below right), 94, 95, 96, 97, 98, 99 (middle right), 100, 102, 104, 106, 108, 109 (below left and right), 110, 111 (below), 112, 113 (below), 114, 115 (top right), 116, 117 (below), 118, 120, 121, 122, 123 (below right), 124 · Jane Pickering 5, 9, 10, 11 (below), 12–13, 14–15, 16, 17, 19, 21, 58 (below right), 60 (top right), 64 (below), 65 (below left), 68 (below), 69 (below), 70 (below), 79 (below), 82 (below), 86 (below), 89 (below left), 94 (below), 103 (below), 114 (top), 118 (below), 121 (below left), 124 (below) · All other illustrations from *The Hamlyn Guide to Trees of Britain and Europe.*

The publishers would like to thank the following organisations and individuals for their kind permission to reproduce the photographs in this book:

Heather Angel/Biophotos 21 · Eric Crichton 5 (right), 95, 112, 118 · Linda Gamlin 6, 7 (left and right), 10, 16, 20 (top and below), 33, 50, 52, 56, 72, 74, 76, 96, 100, 106, 120, 122 · Nature Photographers: 12; Frank Blackburn 88; Brinsley Burbridge 4, 9; Nick Callow 5 (left); Colin Carver 29; Hugh Clark 92; Geoff du Feu 110; Jean Hall 116; E A Janes 18 (top and below), 19 (top and below); David Rae 84; Paul Sterry 44, 48, 80, 104; Anthony Wharton 98 · NHPA: Laurie Campbell 78; J S Gifford 62; Brian Hawkes 59; Walter Murray 77; John Shaw 54; Karl Switak 14; David Woodfall 8 · Zefa Picture Library Cover.